Good news from your neighbours: life-giving rivers from the World Church

Alan Sharp

Sunesis Ministries Ltd

Good news from your poor neighbours: life-giving rivers from the World Church

Published by Sunesis Ministries Ltd
Email: info@stuartpattico.com
Website: www.stuartpattico.com

ISBN 978-0-9930065-1-7

'Loose the bands of wickedness, undo the bundles that oppress, let them that are broken go free, and break asunder every burden.... Then ... thy justice shall go before thy face.... And thou shalt be like a watered garden, and like a fountain of water whose waters shall not fail' (Is. 58: 6, 8, 11).

'(T)hese lepers ... went into one tent, and ate and drank: and they took from thence silver and gold and raiment.... Then they said one to another, "We do not well: for this is a day of good tidings.... (C)ome, let us go and tell it in the king's court"' (2 Kings 7: 8-9).

'Justice (is) ... shorthand for the intention of God, expressed from Genesis to Revelation, to set the whole world right – a plan gloriously fulfilled in Jesus Christ, supremely in his resurrection (following his victory over the powers of evil and death on the cross) and now to be implemented in the world. We cannot get off the hook of present responsibility ... by declaring that the world is currently in such a mess and there's nothing that can be done about it until the Lord returns' (Wright, 2011).

'It is no surprise, then, that most English-speaking people think the New Testament does not say much about justice: the Bibles they read do not say much about justice. English translations are in this way different from translations into Latin, French, Spanish, German, Dutch – and for all I know most languages. The basic issue is well known among translators and commentators. Plato's *Republic*, as we all know, is about justice. The Greek noun in Plato's text that is standardly translated as "justice" is *dikaiosune*.... This same *dik*-stem occurs around three hundred times (233 times, ed.) in the New Testament, in a wide variety of grammatical variants. To the person who comes to the English translation of the New Testament fresh from reading and translating classical Greek, it comes as a surprise to discover that though some of those occurrences are translated with grammatical variants on our word "just" (e.g. justice, ed.), the great bulk of *dik*-stem words are translated with grammatical variants on our word "right" (e.g. righteousness, ed.).... The eighth beatitude reads, "Blessed are those who are persecuted for righteousness' sake, for theirs is the kingdom of heaven" (NRSV) .... My own reading of human affairs is that righteous people are either admired or ignored, not persecuted: people who pursue justice are the ones who get in trouble.... "Righteousness".... in present-day idiomatic English carries a negative connotation. In everyday speech one seldom any more describes someone as *righteous*; if one does, the suggestion is that he (sic) is *self*-righteous. "Justice", by contrast, refers to an interpersonal situation; justice is present when persons are related to each other in a certain way' (Wolterstorff, 2010).

TABLE OF CONTENTS

Table Glossary

Preface

'I have been thinking about the validity ... of a certain set of assumptions conventionally accepted ... as 'knowledge'. This knowledge holds that traditional, canonical American literature is free of, uninformed and unshaped by the four-hundred-year-old presence of, first, Africans and then African-Americans in the United States. It assumes that this presence – which shaped the body politic, the Constitution, and the entire history of the culture – has had no significant place or consequence in the origin and development of the culture's literature.... (A) reason for this is the pattern of thinking about racialism in terms of its consequences on the victim.... That well-established study should be joined with another, equally important one: the impact of racism on those who perpetuate it' (Morrison, 1993; c.f. VanZanten, 2014).

'Then I go to my brother (the white man, ed.)
And I say, "Brother, help me please"
But he winds up knockin' me
Back down on my knees' (Cooke, 1964).

'When anyone ... everywhere commits plunder ... when he distresses the innocent, all cry out, "How long?" ... And this feeling, is it not implanted in us by the Lord? It is then the same as though *God heard himself*, when he hears the cries and groanings of those who cannot bear injustice' (Calvin, 1986, my italics).

In this book I explore what some implications might be of possibly God's biggest work in recent generations: to move the centre of the world church from the West to the Majority World, the people who are the majority of the world. What can we learn from Black, Asian and Latin American Christians and from women generally about God, Jesus, the Bible and life? Does the Bible, for example, help us understand what to do about global injustice? Could there be things that the West has missed and been blind to for generations? Might this even be a matter of life and death?

In this preface I show why white people need to learn from Majority World people, how I developed an anti-racist identity, the realities of oppression and racism and concerns that English Bible translators have downplayed the word 'justice'.

I am a white, modern man. When I make comments about white people, I point the finger at myself first. With respect to my country context, I live in UK, a country where the five richest families have more money than the poorest 20% of the population, or 12.6 million people. Meanwhile, in 2012 nearly three out of every ten people in UK fell below the standard of basic material needs set by UK society as a whole, twice as many people as did so in 1983. With austerity having hit the poorest hardest since 2010 (Oxfam 2014), many Black, Asian and Latin American people in Britain have joined other groups in protesting about how they have been hit hard under austerity (www.thepeoplesassembly.org.uk).

Further, one in ten people in Britain are now millionaires, thanks to the increased market value of their house. So we live among two Britains - the haves and the have nots – which might indicate a considerable level of injustice and that the economic system might not be fit for purpose (Lansley and Mack, 2015). Further, Paul Gilroy (2004) comments that many British people still suffer melancholia or sadness about losing an empire. They try to find one way or another to restore British greatness, as far as they are concerned, by trying to return to the time when Britain had an empire, a more mono-cultural Britain before mass immigration, or by defeating the invader in battle, such as by winning a war abroad, or hoping for any success in sport. Gilroy suggests people should recognise the humanity of people of different ethnic backgrounds so as to go beyond feeling sad at what they've lost. For Western cultural ideology, see ch. 4 of *Changing Generations* (from here called *CG*).

While estimates of Western white people vary between 10 and at most 30% of the world's population (few countries collect these statistics), and even though they are the most powerful people, it is important to identify what the majority of people in the world really think of white people and why. To help us to discover whether our own thinking on different issues has errors in it, Andy Hickford (1998) suggests that we need someone from outside our culture to critique our thinking. Hickford suggests white post-moderns can critique white modern, older people. But this suggestion is limited to white, male younger people, since females are not mentioned.

My research has found that we need women to critique men, and Black, Asian and Latin American people to critique white people because they experience what white people do to them every day. Because of the way that oppression works these people are more likely to convey their critique of white males in what they write than in what they say, since history shows they are more likely to suffer if they say what they think to white people (Haley, 1991). Therefore, in order to provide the best critique of white, male thinking like my own, most of this book is in the words written by women and Black, Asian and Latin American people.

Some Christians may wonder why I'm quoting from a range of people, rather than relying on my own understanding of the Bible. John Stott (1992) emphasises 'double listening': listening to God's word and to non-Christians around you. Mark Noll (1994, 2014), going further, notes the presence of anti-intellectualism at the root of both American white evangelicalism and American democracy generally (c.f. Hofstadter, 1962): a situation perhaps similar to that in UK. The argument with respect to faith goes that faith is not spread by reasoning and learning. Through the action of God, it seems to be that the less educated, less learned people are those who spread the faith. This can encourage the view that ignorance is a better quality than learning.

This leads on to a conviction that the least learned person can answer from the 'Truth' that they have learned when any person comes to them with a view that they do not agree with, without their needing to engage with issues and views in academia and other books that challenge and often disagree with how that Christian might see the issue. One result of this anti-intellectualism is the failure of Christians to engage with the issues people raise who believe differently from how they do, many of which issues are debated in academia. So, movements such as reason, science and secularism have had national and international effects as Christians failed to engage with them, or did so in a way that resulted in more learned people laughing at Christians' reasons for rejecting what to learned people seemed genuine concerns and alternative explanations of what is happening.

Noll calls for a return to the approach of Jonathan Edwards who 350 years ago engaged effectively with academic views that challenged established Christian approaches. We are seeing some responses to this call at last today in that, for example, some of the most famous philosophers alive today, such as Alvin Plantinga and Nicholas Wolterstorff, are Christians, as is Britain's theologian Tom Wright.

I come from a conservative evangelical background, where the focus is on sharing your faith with people who have never heard of Jesus. But the less confessed assumption being made at the same time is that this faith sharing assumes that you are living according to the faith and practice of the Bible. But what if you found out that much of your lifestyle had been built on principles that contradicted the Bible and put other people off from coming to faith (e.g. white supremacy, white privilege, whiteness, white racial identity, see *CG* chs. 4-6)? I spent some time with Black, Asian and Latin American majority churches in London, including trying to learn what was on their agendas. This book eventually arose out of a journey that I took as a result of my work, like many other people, and as shown in the literature (Helms, 1990; Cross, 1991; Thandeka, 1999), in moving from a traditional white racial identity to a white anti-racist identity through a six stage process.

In the pre-contact stage, I saw myself as 'just a British guy'. In the disintegration stage, I saw systematic discrimination by white people against Black, Asian and Latin American people was causing their poverty, unemployment, criminalization, etc. I tried to disassociate myself from white people and wanted Black and Asian people to adopt me. I felt guilt and shame about white oppression and white privilege. In the third stage, that of disintegration, I blamed Black and Asian people for causing their own problems, insisting that they should be able to achieve anything if they tried hard enough. In the fourth stage of being pseudo-independent, I was unsure of how to deal with my white privilege. In stage five, immersion-emersion, I tried to adopt a positive self-concept as a white person who is anti-racist. In the sixth and final stage, autonomy, I emerged from the process having developed a positive white identity based on equality, rather than on superiority, committed to act with people of colour to advocate for justice and empowerment, to dismantle white privilege and work for full inclusion (CG, ch. 5).

To understand how to improve in our learning from Majority World people, it is important to understand what encounters between Western white people and people of Majority World heritage, Black, Asian and Latin American people living in the West, are often like in UK. I was at a discussion in late 2014 about how far people have come in UK in addressing racism. A white person from an anti-racist organization, so some might consider them a 'liberal', thought that UK had come a long way, that there were very few examples of racism occurring today and that Black people shouldn't use race to blame other people if they hadn't done so well economically in UK. As far as gentrification of poor areas was concerned, they understood this as a good thing: that it was primarily the regeneration of an area that had little or no value economically. That through building new homes and developing a new shopping centre, new jobs and prosperity could be brought to an area.

In response, Black people said that to say that there were few examples of racism today in UK displayed the views of middle-class people who were insulated by their lifestyle and socio-economic experience from daily experiences of institutional and grassroots racism. Their experience was that in a recession Black people are the first to be made redundant and the last to be recruited when the economy starts to grow again. That it only took one government to try to ignore and deny the importance of racism for many of the previous gains to be lost (Jasper, 2013).

Black people said they still experience discrimination through police stop and search, through employers being less willing to employ them for jobs that value their skill levels, that their children were more likely to lose heart for self-improvement at school, that people had to fight for fair treatment in mental hospitals, that imprisonment of young Black men is even greater as a proportion of people of their background than in the US (Equality and Human Rights Commission, 2011; National Church Leaders' Forum, 2014). Growing political groups were encouraging people to blame people of other ethnic backgrounds for grievances such as poor job and income prospects for white working class and middle class people and for political parties being out of touch with working class people and making rich people richer at their expense. Black people said people of other ethnic backgrounds shouldn't be blamed for conditions that government policies had themselves made worse.

With respect to gentrification, Black people pointed out the permanent replacement of social housing with a culture of private rented accommodation with rising rents that force poorer people out of the area where their community might have lived for years. When any property comes onto the market it generally is sold to developers who build high cost penthouse type housing on the site that is unaffordable by poorer local people and encourages richer people to move into the area (e.g. Chakrabortty, 2015). There is little sensitivity to the needs of people of different ethnicities for community centres or church buildings that they are allowed to buy where they can meet together for mutual support and development.

What can we learn from this? Most importantly that groups of people of different backgrounds think differently owing to their different socio-economic experience, particularly of oppression. This is human experience of suffering owing to poverty and exploitation. Oppression results from imposition by a dominant minority of social, economic and political arrangements that give that minority continual power over and the ability to impose their way of life on the poorer majority (Ligo, 2000). History shows (*CG*, chs 1-3, 5) that white men naturally oppress people.

The importance of oppression in the Bible is shown in that the very first two stories after the 'fall into sin' seem to highlight ongoing oppression by men against women (Gen. 3: 16-9) and ongoing oppression by men against other men (Gen. 4: 1-16). People who oppress others get a better standard of living than oppressed people by making those oppressed people poorer, and therefore oppressors develop a different way of seeing life from how oppressed people see life. So on many issues many white men think differently from white women, many middle-class people think differently from working class people and many white people think differently from Black, Asian and Latin American people. If you are oppressed, you also have the benefit of double consciousness (Du Bois, 1989). There comes a point when most Majority World people realize that white people are closing off to them most of their opportunities in life. In response, they develop double consciousness. This means that you understand what oppressors think on any subject, as well as what you think about it. This helps you protect yourself, as you can tell oppressors what they want to hear, but it can result in psychological pressures on the oppressed, unless they have developed the mental strength to overcome these pressures.

So for many white people, race, for example, is no longer seen as an obstacle to economic progress while racism is not intrinsic to unjust structures of society but is limited to hate crimes committed by a small number of people who are prejudiced. This is a 'colour-blind', cultural form of racism, where Black and Asian participation as British citizens is accepted bearing in mind that they are seen as inferior for various cultural reasons (e.g. Black people are not good at school but are good at sport, Muslims can't be trusted, Asians love family life and business) (Mirza, 2005). For white people generally, in the 'colour-blind' society, people should not see and hence should not discuss 'race', since 'we are all equal'. If someone does bring up racism, therefore, they may well be accused of 'playing the race card', of being racist, or too 'politically correct' (Doane, 2003). At the same time, much white racism comes from people's unconscious unmet desires, which means making effective interventions to stop racism can be challenging (Bhavnani, Mirza and Meetoo, 2005).

Black and Asian working class people, however, can tell people about racism that they suffer daily. The reason is because they have experienced it (Kwaku, 2014). The official white approved way of using social sciences is to use a scientific, objective research process to establish whether, for example, racism or sexism is happening. If you experience racism or sexism, however, this might appear to trump whether someone can prove by scientific objectivity whether racism or sexism is happening or not, since it's very difficult to prove that any research was objective when it's so difficult to keep personal subjective opinion and action from biasing the research findings (Alkalimat, 1998; CG, ch. 6).

The experiences that Black people go through are used by them to help them to interpret the Bible, which is the basis of Black theology (Reddie, 2014). Asian and Latin American peoples do similarly with their own experiences. White people insist that they just do what the Bible says, and that their interpretations are unaffected by their socio-economic experience and unconscious assumptions. Unfortunately, it seems that they are in denial about this. For example, how does a person know that they are not using their unconscious assumptions when interpreting the Bible, since those assumptions are unconscious? Further, white people do not complain that the Bible appears to say so little about justice, since they get so much in life through their experience of white privilege, without praying for things they need. However, Black people keep looking in the Bible and keep praying for how they can get change and get justice, since many so often suffer from unjust treatment.

Some people have said that they would not buy my book Changing Generations, preferring to wait for 'the book for Christians'. Could I encourage everyone to read CG first in order properly to understand this book? The two books go together. The approaches and findings in CG are often rarely, if at all, dealt with in church, yet all of them are relevant for Christians. I could not duplicate that approach in this book, sadly, without making this book impossibly long and expensive.

I am here using the Douay Rheims version of the Bible, unless otherwise stated. This is not to claim that this is the best, all-round version of the Bible. I do not accept as canonical those books which are not part of the Hebrew Bible. Voth (2003) highlights concerns about English version translators' preference for translating the Hebrew word sedeq primarily as 'righteousness' rather than 'justice' (see ch. 7 below). See also the comments on English language translations in both Old and New Testaments by Orlando Costas (1989). Wolterstorff (2010 and 2013) shows that while dikaiosune means 'justice' in ancient Greek, such as in Plato's

Republic (see *CG*, ch. 4), most English version NT translators translate *dikaiosune* often as 'righteousness' (c.f. Lee, 2014). The Douay Rheims uses the word 'justice' more frequently – 310 times - than any other English version I have found. Standard versions in languages other than English, together with newer versions like the Nueva Version Internacional (1999) in Spanish, produced mainly by evangelicals, use the word 'justice' even more frequently than the Douay Rheims, but I have yet to find English translations of these versions. The careful reader will note that there are sometimes verse number differences between Roman Catholic and Protestant versions. I have used Protestant version verse numbers.

I thank those who taught me so much on *CG*: Michael Williams, Cindy Soso, Sam Amalemba, Richard Reddie, Israel Olofinjana, Anne Bowyer, Marika Sherwood, Michael Ohajuru. Also Sue Jelfs and Jenny Dyke and their students.

To my family, Abbi and Tim, Evan and Rach, Mel and Zac, Fran and Andy, thanks for all your suggestions and your patience with my being distracted. To Norma, thank you so much for your patience and love while I have been so mentally pre-occupied!

Tom Chacko has been my mentor. Any inspiration here comes from him. The mistakes, however, are mine alone.

Introduction - Laying my cards on the table

'A person is not only a sinner, a person is also the sinned-against.... (M)en and women are not only willful violators of God's laws, they are also the violated. This is not to be understood in a behaviouristic sense, but in a theological sense, in terms of sin, the domination of sin.... (M)an is lost, lost not only in the sins in his own heart but also in the sinning grasp of principalities and powers of the world, demonic forces which cast a bondage over human lives and human institutions and infiltrate their very textures. Because of our involvement with the poor, we discover that a person persistently deprived of basic material needs and political rights is also a person deprived of much of his or her soul - self-respect, dignity and will' (Fung, 1980).

'Émile Durkheim (1967) ... warned against this phenomenon (individualism that promotes theologies that cause people to retreat into a comfort zone, where their spirituality is measured by their "righteous state of being", ed.). He pointed out that religion was occupying a smaller and smaller portion of social life. Originally, religion played a significant role in all areas of life. However, slowly but surely, the political, economic, and scientific worlds separated themselves from their religious functions. Durkheim observed that, "God ... who at the beginning was present in all human relations, now progressively withdraws, abandoning the world to men and their conflicts." The result is that religion is then reduced to the private life of individuals. In evangelical terms, the transforming power of the gospel is taken away from the public sphere and is reduced and limited to a privatized expression' (Voth, 2003).

In this chapter, I explain why salvation includes building for God's kingdom in this life, how Jesus' life shows we can reconcile with people we have oppressed, and how this links with global inequality. I conclude with an outline of the book.

Rethinking salvation – duality v. holism

Tom Wright (2011) is a modern-day theologian who has engaged with many concerns that people have raised about Christian faith. Apparently, while many church leaders are privately enthusiastic about what he has said, many become fearful of implementing his suggestions because they fear what their churches and denominational bosses might say. Wright says that the works of Jesus, for example his healings and causing people who were considered of low social status to be accepted as equals by people of higher status, demonstrate Jesus was showing us what we should be doing as part of renewing creation.

Wright demonstrates that a range of themes is used in the NT showing that God intends to remake creation, having dealt with the evil that is distorting it through the victory of the resurrection of Christ. In 1 Corinthians 15 Paul speaks of Jesus being the first-fruits of the resurrection. In the same chapter he also speaks of Jesus submitting all powers in the cosmos to himself, like a king destroying his enemies. In Philippians 3: 20-1, Paul speaks of believers as the citizens of heaven. Jesus will come from heaven to earth to transform their bodies by resurrection as part of his bringing all things into subjection to himself.

Returning to 1 Corinthians 15, in v. 28 Paul speaks of God being 'all in all'. Anticipating the 'new creation' passage in Isaiah 65 and 66, the prophet speaks in Is. 11 of 'the earth is filled with the knowledge of the Lord'. In Romans 8: 18-27 we see that the whole creation is waiting on tiptoe for God's children to be revealed, whose resurrection will herald creation's new life. Using the theme of new birth, new creation is born from the womb of the old creation. Further, from John, in Revelation 20-21 we see the marriage of heaven and earth, the church itself coming down from heaven to earth and the remaking of the whole creation.

Jesus has now gone to heaven, from where he is ruling the world and interceding with the Father for us, but has come to be with his people by the Spirit. How will human beings contribute towards the remaking of the world? Jesus' work in healing, delivering people from oppression, raising the dead, etc. was up close and personal examples of what he promised long-term in the future. It was not about saving souls so they could have a disembodied eternity, but rescuing people from the evil and decay of the current world, so that in the present they could both enjoy that renewal of creation and also become partners in God's long-term larger project of renewing creation on earth, the place where Jesus was resurrected. Paul says we should always be abounding in the work of the Lord (1 Cor. 15: 58). He was saying that the works done in our bodies are important even though our bodies will die. It is part of building for God's kingdom.

When we think about mission, we find that for some people, mission means 'going to heaven when you die', whereas for others it means, 'doing justice and peace in this world'. The 'this world bad/next world good' (e.g. evangelical) or vice versa (e.g. liberal) options show the effect of the either/or duality of Greek Platonism on Western Christianity and civilization. By contrast, the NT speaks of salvation as 'being raised to life in God's new heaven and new earth'. Humanity's mandate since Genesis was to bring order to God's world and maintain communities: salvation is not just for a person's private benefit. So, salvation should be about whole people, not just souls; about the present, not just the future; and about God doing things through us, rather than in and for us.

The 'kingdom of heaven' is the rule of God in heaven breaking into this world of earth. So the resurrection and God's gift of the Spirit were designed not to take us away from the decaying earth to heaven, but to help us transform the earth in anticipation of God's new creation of the cosmos. So in redeeming God's created world, we need to start with justice, righting earthly injustice so as to respect the image of God in other people. This should include prioritising healing the sick, supporting the weak, sharing the faith, caring for the environment, so that God's will is done on earth as it is in heaven.

Rethinking reconciliation – embracing people different from ourselves
Wright (1996) says that the reformers focused very much on Jesus' death and resurrection when formulating their theology, rather than on Jesus' incarnation and life to that point. Wright shows this theology to be ahistorical and also abstract. Reddie (2014) points out that Paul's letters began to be written a generation before the earliest gospels and that Paul also focuses on Jesus' passion, death and resurrection and tends not to refer as much, on balance, to Jesus' life and ministry.

Reddie says that Jesus' life and ministry, for example in how he engaged with the Samaritan woman and the Syrophoenician woman, undercuts any ideas of gender, ethnic, cultural or national prejudice. Jesus taught that we should love both God (vertical relationship) and our neighbour as ourselves (horizontal relationship). This was a cross-shaped formula for reconciliation. Western white Christians have downplayed the concrete life and ministry of Jesus, appearing to follow Paul and the reformers in this, and have used their focus on the spiritual and the abstract to justify ignoring the material and physical.

White evangelicals have taught us to worship Christ but not to follow his collective prophetic action. They have focused on vertical reconciliation with God and used their acceptance with God to justify ignoring their responsibilities towards their neighbour. They have then tended to take their values on engagement with their neighbour, sadly, from the prevailing secular thinking of the day. Anyone who is different from the white, middle-class male has had to put up with the consequences to themselves. This has included action like chattel enslavement of Black people, support for white supremacy and economic exploitation of the Majority World.

As early as the Nicene and Apostles' Creeds, a spiritualization of the central beliefs of Christianity had taken place. The creeds tell us about Jesus' salvation and atonement, but nothing about the liberating actions of his life and ministry. The creedal statements of Jesus' death and resurrection are shorn of the counter-cultural praxis of his life that explains why his death was both inevitable and redemptive.

Black people's approach to reconciliation is based on Jesus' life rather than on his death. Jesus was a Jew, a people that throughout their history were oppressed, both nationally and internationally (see ch. 6 below). Wright (1996) shows that Jesus contextualized his ministry for second Temple exile Jews, who were looking for a greater liberation from exile, having lived since their return under the control of several external powers. Jesus underwent oppression throughout much of his life. The fact that Jesus was oppressed shows God's taking the form of oppressed people in order to show God siding with oppressed people in their suffering. So oppressed people see God identifying with them, and in God's doing so see God as Black, Asian, Latin American, etc.

When Jesus meets with Zacchaeus (Luke 19: 1-10), Jesus calls for and commends an ethic of reparations to reconcile between oppressors and the oppressed and with God. Zacchaeus is to give back what he has wrongly taken to be reconciled to the people he has oppressed and to God. This is a Biblical take on restorative justice.

Sadly, when emancipation came from enslavement, Black people received not a penny in reparations, while white slave planters received a fortune in compensation. However, to think that this was all 200 years ago with little relevance to today could not be further from the truth (see ch. 4).

Global injustice – the cry of your poor neighbours

It would be useful, if it were possible, to do a survey of everyone in the world to see what was the greatest problem or injustice that they were struggling with. A number of writers have identified the level of injustice both within and between countries (e.g. Stuart, 2009; Wilkinson and Pickett, 2010). Paul Hawken (2007) has dubbed today's global justice movement as 'the largest social movement in history'.

The West appears to be living in luxury every day, while the Majority World is surviving on scraps. Reddie explains that Jesus tells his followers to see God's image in the lives of the disparaged 'Other', the neighbour, 'these least brethren', (Matt. 25. 31-46). How at the last judgment are white evangelicals to answer Jesus for being complicit in injustice? What, for example, can we make of the ritualized destruction of Black bodies during lynching on trees across the US well into the twentieth century, often by 'good Christian white folk' (Pinn, 2003; Cone, 2013)?

Where this book is going

If I have concerns about Christian faith today, it is about how people not only address the real issues for the majority of the world today from the guidance in the Bible, but also how they can use this to lay a basis for an alternative future (Pregeant, 1978).

In this book I try to explore what God might be saying through moving the centre of the church from the North Atlantic to the Majority World. I start each chapter with a brief outline of the chapter. I outline the daily economic system that the West has imposed on the Majority World and explain how people from the Majority World understand it from the Bible. I look at the rise of the church in the Majority World and some challenges facing the church in the West. I explore the interaction of Western Christian missionaries with people from the Majority World over the last three centuries. I focus on the psychological damage that white Europeans did to African people during 400 years of enslavement throughout the Western Hemisphere and subsequently that is severely impacting many in those communities to this day, including those who have migrated to UK. I show how white people's exploitation of Black, Asian and Latin American people worldwide caused white people to become the global rich.

This leads into an exploration of the Bible doctrines of oppression and justice as they are understood by many Majority World Christians. In the light of what the Bible says, we leave the reader with the question, 'Can the global rich get to heaven?'

Part One – Western engagement with people from the Majority World

Chapter 1
The West's economic system that is killing the Majority World

'People know about the Klan and the overt racism, but the killing of one's soul little by little, day after day, is a lot worse than someone coming in your house and lynching you' (Jackson, 2011).

'Frank (Frank Marshall Davis, at the time a well-known poet, ed.) said, "Stan's (Obama's grandfather: Obama was living with his white grandparents at the time, ed.) basically a good man. But he doesn't *know* me. He *can't* know me, not the way I know him. Maybe some of these Hawaiians can, or the Indians (indigenous peoples, ed.) on the reservation. They've seen their fathers humiliated. Their mothers desecrated. But your grandfather will never know what that feels like. That's why he can come over here and drink my whiskey and fall asleep in that chair.... That's something I can never do in his house. *Never.* Doesn't matter how tired I get, I still have to watch myself. I have to be vigilant, for my own survival.... Your grandma's right to be scared (she had recently been threatened by a black man, ed.).... She understands that black people have a reason to hate. That's just how it is. For your sake I wish it were otherwise. But it's not. So you might as well get used to it".... I walked back to the car. The earth shook under my feet, ready to crack open at any moment. I stopped, trying to steady myself, and knew for the first time that I was utterly alone' (Obama, 2007).

'Neoliberal capitalism not only produces dreams and hopes but itself... promulgates a utopia: the utopia of a world completely dominated by the logic of the market. In a horizon founded on the desire of consumption, there is no significant place for the suffering of the poor and socially excluded. When they "cross" that horizon they are seen as intruders, and end up being ignored, expelled, or even exterminated' (Sung, 2011).

Here I explain that Western people's ability to choose their favourite consumer product requires that Majority World people struggle to get life's basic necessities. Many in the Majority World understand this as idolatry. We look at this through Marx's critique of capitalism and what the Bible says.

    This chapter fits naturally after chapters 3 and 4 of *CG*. These deal with the growth of economic inequality between developed and underdeveloped countries and the West's cultural ideology and behaviour towards people of the Majority World. People from a Majority World background living in the West are treated the same way by white people in the West as people from their original country background.

The justification by faith that Paul speaks of in Rom. 3: 21-6 transforms people into those who can do justice, 'Present… your members as instruments of justice unto God' (Rom. 6: 13). Today, the exclusion of Gentiles by Jews, spoken of in Gal. 3: 28, might no longer be an issue for believers. However, today we need to consider exclusion for economic, political and cultural reasons as a live issue for everyone.

What the West is involved in today is accumulation of possessions and enabling Western people to have their product preferences through the mechanisms of neo-liberal globalization, including structures like the World Trade Organisation (WTO), the World Bank (WB), the IMF and transnational corporations. The project of helping people in a consumer society to select their favourite brands excludes by its design a vast number of people worldwide. This is as an alternative to working to ensure most people in the world get their basic material needs. See Lansley and Mack (2015) for a UK list of basic material needs. Accumulation of possessions while the poor do not have access to basic material needs is seen as idolatry by the Majority World.

Elsa Tamez (1993) says that the primary concern of Latin Americans at the time of her writing was, 'the premature death that is imposed today on the people who live in poor nations, and the affirmation of the God of life and Liberator who opts for the poor'. Tamez says that justification by faith can be seen as an answer to psychological dehumanization that leaves you with guilt feelings and craving for approval as a human before God. By comparison, Tamez points to the corporal, social and cultural dehumanization that people from the Majority World experience as a result of malnutrition and insignificance.

People suffering from hunger and insignificance are more at risk of dying. Sin is granted legitimacy through the exclusion of people from the system's benefits. What is at stake is an idol which imposes itself as sovereign. Sin kills the excluded people.

The world's economic system proclaims the opposite to justification by faith: justification by merit. The system, based on productivity and white privilege, proclaims salvation by the law of maximum profit, through the privatization of production of goods and services. With this salvation being achieved by merit, based on economic, cultural and social criteria of worthiness, many people remain outside and are lost. These people are the condemned of the earth. Ultimately, though, the powerful become dehumanized themselves, as a result of killing other people.

The facts speak for themselves. Britain and the West increased their wealth principally by taking the labour, land and resources of the Majority World for far less than what they were worth. The ratio of income per person in developed countries vs. income per person in developing countries grew from 3:1 in 1820 to 72:1 in 1992 (UNDP, 1999). That is, on average, people in developed countries earn and live on over 70 times as much money every day as people in developing countries. Today 20% of the world consumes 76.6% of its private consumption, while 70% of the world consumes just 15.3% of the world's private consumption. Almost half the world, or over 3 billion people, live on less than 2.50 US dollars a day. 21,000 children under the age of 5 die every day from preventable illnesses. Nearly a billion people cannot read a book or sign their name. 12% of the world uses 85% of its water: none of that 12% lives in the Majority World. 1.1 billion people in developing countries have inadequate access to water and 2.6 billion people lack adequate sanitation. 1.6 billion people live without electricity. 790 million people in the developing world are chronically undernourished. In 1970 the world's 60 poorest countries owed 25 billion US dollars in debt. By 2002, after paying off 550 billion US dollars, their outstanding debt had risen to 523 billion US dollars. Subsequent headline-grabbing promises by rich countries' world leaders for Majority World debt cancellation have hardly been kept. For every 1 dollar a developing country receives in aid (Moyo, 2010), over 25 dollars are spent on debt repayment (Global Issues website).

The elaborate system that Western governments, non-governmental organisations and transnational corporations and mainly white people have put in place to keep this international injustice working in their favour is explained throughout *CG*. Many aspects are financial and international (e.g. IMF structural adjustment programmes (SAPs) that have caused inequality and poverty to rise in many countries), but others relate to philosophy (e.g. violence towards 'the cultural Other'), psychology (e.g. white identity, whiteness), sociology (e.g. racism, sexism, classism), etc.

To explain the current system and why many from the Majority World see this as idolatry that people need liberation from, we turn initially to Franz Hinkelammert, a white Christian economist who has spent many years in Latin America. Hinkelammert (2006) sees Thomas Hobbes as being the first person to theorise about bourgeois society, where a pseudo-divine world towers above humans. For Hobbes, the king, or sovereign, has the legitimacy to repress people. Hobbes called bourgeois society Leviathan: money is the blood of the Leviathan. Later theorists, including Adam Smith and Max Weber have indicated that the central object of devotion is the machinery of goods (described here as 'commodities'), money, market and capital. One virtue is pre-eminent: humility, which causes you to submit to the object of devotion and never rebel. John Locke said the worst thing to do was to oppose the capitalist system, and that people who do should suffer torture, slavery and death. Hinkelammert (1986) uses Marx's analysis to explain how the machinery of the system works.

The commodity fetish

Marx (1977) says that something that a worker produces meets a need, therefore it has a use-value. However, it becomes important to both the seller and buyer for its exchange-value, its price. This exchange turns the product into a commodity. Although the product was useful, the reason for producing it now becomes its exchange value and the fact that it is now a commodity. This word 'commodity' is broader than materials that are traded on a commodity exchange. Commodity here refers to any product that has been sold.

Marx says commodities take on 'metaphysical' qualities. It is the commodity that is spoken about, not the people who made it. Commodities set up social relationships between each other in different ways, particularly on the stock exchange and on international money markets. Oil fights coal. Plastic fights wood. Iron and steel are paired together. So the commodity's producer gets dominated by the commodity and not vice versa. We might recall how many Majority World economies were left by colonialists at independence with their exports dominated by a single commodity (Kidron and Segal, 1981).

If your income as a country is dependent on export of a single commodity that then suffers from conditions outside your country's control, your economy can be sunk. Prices for coffee, plastics and steel are dependent on fluctuations on the stock market. Oil prices are governed by supply and demand, which in turn can be based on guesses based on human behaviour, rational or irrational, and the production process. Commodities start to move and are beyond human control. The social relationships of commodities make it seem as if they were persons beyond the control of real people. In this they can, for example, be joined together 'in marriage' with other products within merged companies, or by their sales collapsing they can contribute towards people who labour to produce the commodities losing their jobs. So objects take on life and subjectivity, which is the life of people projected onto them, while people are transformed into things.

What do we mean by 'fetishism'? A fetish is an object that has supernatural powers, or an object made by people that has power over others. The analysis of fetishism we are dealing with here is concerned with the spirit of the material institutions that organize today's society. We need to recognise that a social division of labour is imposed on everyone. Fetishism is concerned with the type of social division of labour that tends to make invisible, or to hide, the effect of that social division of labour on the life or death of people.

Commodity relationships make it appear that people's interpersonal relationships are independent of how the division of labour affects people's survival. That the fact that a commodity's collapse, for example, that results in someone losing their job is independent of and unrelated to the business decision that certain business people took to make that person unemployed. Commodity relationships make it appear that these are the 'rules of the game', that 'the market did it', whereas in fact they are the rules of a life and death struggle between people. The action of making a person producing the product that became a commodity redundant is the work of business people who should be made responsible for the results of their actions.

People put into commodities their dreams and hopes, their longings and fears, as a result of the fact that they have been alienated from the product of their labour. So a Nike shoe is not seen as a rubber/plastic component that is overpriced related to its labour cost, but something people need to buy to feel better about themselves by giving them a status among their peers.

Not only are people saying the market is responsible rather than business people. They are also saying that conditions are God-given, as if they are a fact of life. People cannot afford to live because the market says there have to be poor people. The world has been turned upside down since the economic process has taken responsibility for human interactions. Health care happens not based on human need, but whether money is available. When responsibility for humans is given to the market, this must be idolatry.

The money fetish

Hinkelammert explains that for Marx, money is the commodity above all commodities and is the common denominator between commodities. Money is the master of the world of commodities, since money converts all products into commodities. Through money, Marx says that commodities are brought into opposition to each other, and are ruled over by money, since with the same money one can buy one commodity rather than another. So humans, with their lives already ruled over by commodities, are now ruled over by the transcendent commodity, money. Marx therefore calls money the 'Mark of the Beast', quoting Rev. 13: 17; and 17: 13.

Commodities think for humans and also tell them the laws governing their behaviour. So commodities think up money. Humans then confirm the thought through creating money. The fact that money is qualitatively independent of all limits, yet its quantity is limited, drives people to hoard by wealth accumulation. See ch. 3 of *CG* for comparison of the wealth of different groups within UK. Accumulation or hoarding is a precondition to having access to everything. Work, thrift and greed become a person's three main virtues, selling much and buying little. The fetish of money becomes the object of devotion.

The capital fetish

Richard and Vidales, in their introduction to Hinkelammert's book, say that as money becomes transformed into capital, that itself is transformed physically into machines, commodity relationships have the decision over whether the producer dies or lives. Capital is the accumulation of surplus value. A worker is now completely dependent on commodities. If oil prices go up, an airline worker may become redundant owing to higher refueling costs, while an oil rig worker may get a raise owing to higher profits. The worker must be kept alive but companies are only concerned about giving the worker the bare essentials. The capitalist becomes a machine for transforming surplus value into capital.

Those who believe free markets are best to create free societies ignore what has happened since Adam Smith. As service got physically separated from where the exchange got made, and commodities and money relationships became more impersonal, the market became more interested in accumulation of capital and less interested in how human beings benefit. So suicides have increased in India among peasant farmers, for example, as a result of crops of the type that they had been growing being dumped by transnational corporations at below their cost levels on the Indian economy. Capital then consumes land, so that farmers are no longer dependent on their own work in the sustenance economy, but rather on the 'money economy' (Is. 3: 14b-15). In 1991, Nike paid an average Indonesian woman worker 0.82 dollars a day, charged customers 100 times that per pair of shoes, and paid Michael Jordan 20 million dollars, that is, more than they paid all workers in Indonesia (Rourke, 1996).

Capital fetishism portrays capital as being the source of infinite gains for humans. Capital, however, takes its life from the human beings who operate the machines, and thereby sows death in the earth.

Alternative economic systems

When we see that the market depends on decisions of workers, managers and owners, undisguised by the social relationships between commodities, we can move away from market idolatry and take back our responsibility for economic structures in our society. If we take part in economic decision-making, we can move towards implementing a system where production benefits everyone, rather than just a few.

Some examples of alternative economic systems are shown in CG, chapters 9 and 10. Duchrow and Hinkelammert (2004), for example, show how different kinds of property can be redefined for the benefit of the common good, so that people can all have the basic material needs of life.

Idolatry in the Bible

Pablo Richard (2006) says there are three types of idolatry in the Bible. In the first type, in the example of the Hebrews choosing the golden calf rather than Moses' leadership in Exod. 32, the people were rejecting God's action of liberation from slavery, in favour of a god who would lead them back to Egypt where they would continue in slavery. In the second type, the Hebrews wanted to worship other gods who were believed to exist in their own lands. In the OT the most common instances relate to the kings of Israel: wealth, power and idolatry went together, including injustice to the poor. Deut. 17: 14-20 forbids kings from building military power, accumulation of silver and gold and having many women, as this related to polytheism.

The third type of idolatry occurs in a context of political oppression. In 2 Kings 25: 24, Gedaliah tells the Jews that they should trust the king of Babylon and serve him, so liberation is found by submitting to power. However, Jeremiah says, in the same context, for the Jews not to be afraid of the king of Babylon, because God is able to save them from him (Jer. 42: 11). Babylonian people made idols to materialize the power of the king of Babylon. In Is. 40-55, under Babylonian oppression, God encourages the Jews to resist Babylonian power and their gold and silver gods, because God will carry and bring liberation to the Jews.

In the NT, we find four groups of passages treating different aspects of idolatry. First, idolatry that is destructive of people, nature and history. In Acts 17: 16-34 in Athens, Paul radicalizes OT teaching on idolatry. Paul says that God does not need idols in order to be revealed, and also people do not need idols in order to know God. Through God's liberating work in history people can now know God by faith. Idols, however, destroy history, people and nature, so that people make fetishes or idols in order to use them against other people. If people are made in the image of God, then no spirituality can be revealed through the destruction of humans' lives.

Further, idolatry of money. We find the following equivalences:

- idiolater/usurer/swindler/thief (1Cor. 5: 9-13; 6: 9-11)
- idolatry/feuding/wrangling/jealousy/belligerence/envy (Gal. 5: 20-1)
- idolatry and greed are synonymous in Eph: 5: 5 and Col. 3: 5.

With greed comes the desire to extract more money from other people, bringing discord. Idolatry is someone's submission to the power of money. In Matt. 6: 24 Jesus says we cannot serve God and Mammon (money).

Again, there is idolatry of the law. We find from Gal. 4: 8-11 that when someone looks to the law as a means for their salvation, the law becomes an idol that kills them. The law creates a non-liberating hope of salvation. In Mark 2: 1-3: 2 Jesus develops a theology that is anti-idolatry, opposing the law. He says, 'The sabbath was made for man, and not man for the sabbath'. Idolatry of the law perverts people's consciences, destroying their political, social and personal relationships.

Finally, there is the idolatry of oppressive power of the state. In Rev. 13-17 and 19 we read of the idolatry of 'the beast'. People who do not wear a sign of submission to the beast on their body cannot buy or sell anything. Early Christians opposed the Roman emperor in their being worshipped as a god, affirming their liberation in Jesus Christ.

In the Majority World today, as elsewhere in the world, people are crushed by the idols of an oppressive economic system. Because capitalism is idolatrous rather than atheistic, it poses theological and political issues for people. This is a type of situation that did not take place during Bible times. It requires today that people engage in the praxis of liberation, that demands the transformation of the political and economic structure of an idolatrous system.

Chapter 2
Rise of the World Church: challenges for the Western Church

'At the start of the twenty-first century, Christianity has become the most global of all religions and its radically changed manifestation in the world has turned it into a predominantly "non-Western religion", to the extent that it has now ceased to be shaped primarily by the events and processes at work in Western culture' (Bediako, 2005).

'If it were not for Black churches that are able to hold the people together, to give some sense of value at work and to make them feel that God is on our side, they (Black people) would all be in mental institutions. And when I myself as a Methodist minister feel very low, and I mean really low, I do not go to a Methodist church to uplift me. I go for spiritual upliftment to what I know I will never get from any white preacher' (Revd. Hewlette (Hewie) Andrew, 1990).

Here I outline growth in the church worldwide since 1970. I use my research in Tooting, South London to show how Majority World church growth is impacting some urban areas in UK. I compare forms of evangelicalism, including Pentecostalism, between Black, Asian and Latin American and white people in the West. I note differences owing to Western dualism, the inability of the West to contextualize their faith in recent centuries and different approaches towards ecumenism.

Growth of the Church in the Majority World, 1970-2020
Table 1. Proportions of church in Majority World and the West, 1970-2020 (Source: World Christian Database, 2013)

	1970	2010	2020 forecast
All Christians (millions)	1229	2263	2551
% in Majority World	41.6	61.3	65.2
% in West	58.4	38.7	34.8
All evangelicals (millions)	95	285	349
% in Majority World	37.4	74.8	78.1
% in West	62.6	25.2	21.9

Table 2. Renewalists (millions) (Source: World Christian Database, 2013)

	1970	2010	2020 forecast
Pentecostals in denominations	15	92	115
Charismatics in denominations	4	234	282
Charismatics outside denominations	44	257	313
	----	----	----
Total renewalists	63	583	710
	====	====	====

Table 3. Christians by continent (millions) (Source: World Christian Database, 2013).

	1970	2010	2020 forecast
Africa	143	488	631
Asia	95	348	420
Latin America/Caribbean	270	542	601
Pacific excl. Aust/NZ	3	9	11
	----	----	----
Total Majority World	511	1387	1663
North America	211	279	288
Europe	492	578	580
Australia/New Zealand	15	19	20
	----	----	----
Total in West	718	876	888
	----	----	----
Christians in world	1229	2263	2551
	====	====	====

While all major streams of Christianity have been increasing in the Majority World since 1970, one example of a faster rate of growth has been the growth of evangelicals. In 1970, nearly 60% of all evangelicals lived in the West. By 2010, 60% of all churchgoers and almost ¾ of all evangelicals lived in Majority World countries.

Further, during 1970-2010, Renewalists grew at four times the growth of both Christianity and the world's population. Renewalists include Pentecostals and Charismatics within denominations and Charismatics outside of denominations. Many renewalists are evangelical, but many are not.

Of the implications of such changes in the centre of Christianity, Lamin Sanneh (2003 and 2008) writes, 'Christianity from its origin was marked by serial retreat and advance as an intercultural process. Bethlehem and Jerusalem were superseded by Antioch and Athens, while Egypt and Carthage soon gave place to

Rome. Rival centres multiplied the chances of further contraction and expansion. Then it was the turn of the North Atlantic to inherit the mantle before the next momentous phase brought the religion to the Southern Hemisphere, with Africa representing the most recent continental shift. (For map showing movements in centre of gravity, see Barrett and Johnson (2003) ed.) These developments went beyond merely adding more names to the books; they had to do with *cultural shifts*, with *changing the books themselves*. This serial feature of the history of Christianity is largely hidden from people in the West now living in a post-Christian culture' (my italics).

So, with the majority of Christians now being Black, Asian and Latin American, we not only need to hear the insights God has given them about God, but also their views expressed in their books on how white people might better live their lives to do God's will. Further, if Christian unity means anything, there needs to be a partnership between white, Black, Asian and Latin American Christians in working locally, nationally and internationally for God.

The evidence is that growth of the church was remarkably slow during the last two centuries of European mission. In 1900, all Protestants in the Majority World totaled 4 million, out of a world population of 1.62 billion (Johnstone, 1998: Barrett and Johnson, 2001/2). Patrick Johnstone sees the growth, which has largely taken place since 1960 (i.e. since independence), as taking place primarily in Africa in the 1960s, in Latin America in the 1970s, in East Asia in the 1980s and in Eurasia in the 1990s.

Dana Robert (2000) recognizes that this explosive growth happened when Christian missionaries were not looking and after colonizers and Western denominational missionaries had withdrawn. Crucial to the growth was the existence of indigenous churches that were independent from Western denominations.

It is estimated that at the time of the Communist takeover in China in 1949, already a quarter of all Chinese Christians were in such independent indigenous churches and hence were more able to resist Communist domination. Just 700,000 Protestants in China in 1949 grew to between 12 and 36 million by 2000.

African Indigenous or Independent Churches (AICs) had grown since the 1880s. Christianity grew in the 1960s under indigenous leadership, including in Western-origin denominations. The largest group of AICs was Spirit churches in East Africa, Aladura in West Africa and Zionist in southern Africa. These churches focus on healing of spirit and body, laying on of hands and other gifts of the Spirit, but also on evangelism and preaching. By 1984 we find 7,000 AIC denominations in 43 African countries. By 1990, 40% of African Christians in South Africa attended AICs.

In Latin America the growth of Base Christian Communities doing Bible study and developing a more intense spirituality put pressure on a Roman Catholic

Church already short of clergy. New churches have begun outside traditional denominations. Pentecostals are now at their strongest in Latin America. Universal Church of the Kingdom of God, based in Brazil, numbers six million adherents worldwide. Christianity in the Majority World supports community and family life in a context of economic hardship and political uncertainty, through grassroots leadership, a reliance on the Bible and embeddedness in local cultures (Brock, 2005).

To understand the nature of this growth, we can consider Anglicans, who are the third largest Christian denomination worldwide, following the Orthodox and Roman Catholic churches. George Carey (2006) says that while the average English Anglican is a woman in her middle 50s who is comfortably off, the average Anglican worldwide is a young Black woman with at least two children, living on less than 2 dollars a day, semi-literate and having someone in her family who suffers from Aids/HIV. If this 'average Anglican' is similar to 'average world Christians', then, following Lamin Sanneh's comment above, how does this woman's experience of Jesus and her theology and missiology change people's understanding of what God is saying in the 21st century? To answer this question, I look at the characteristics of evangelicalism in the West before considering the characteristics of evangelicalism in the Majority World. We start by looking at issues arising from the presence of Majority World Christians in UK in Tooting, in inner city South London.

Case study: Tooting – the world in microcosm
In 2012, churchgoers in London by ethnicity were white 53%, Black 28%, Asian 12%, mixed 5%, other non-white (e.g. Latin American) 2% (Brierley, 2012). Bearing in mind the large number of European immigrants attending churches, it might not be surprising if the proportion of white British churchgoers was now in a minority in London. In Inner London, including Wandsworth borough where Tooting is located, churchgoers are white 38%, Black 48% and others 14%.

Table 4 Evangelical and Pentecostal churches in Tooting, London SW17 (Sharp research, quoted in Wilkinson, 2005).

P	Church name	White	Black	Asian	Latin American	Total	Own Premises	Rent	Language other than English
Ca	New Test. Assembly		1000			1000	/		
G	SW London Ghana SDA		210			210		/	
G	Methodist	10	180			190	/		
Ca	Yahweh CF	10	170			180	/		
W	Trinity Rd Chapel	145	20	5		170	/		
Ca	Lynwood CF		150			150	/		
Ca	New Testament COG		150			150	/		
B	Igreja Mana				130	130		/	/
Ca	Pilgrims Union COG		120			120	/		
SL	Zion COG			110		110		/	/
Ca	Tooting Junction BC	15	90			105	/		
W	St. Nicholas	60	30	10		100	/		
G	Victory Baptist		100			100		/	
F	Life in the Spirit	15	5	80		100	/		
W	HTB 3 pastorates	90				90	/		
Co	Rock of Ages CA		80			80		/	/
Ma	Victorious CC		5	75		80		/	/
G	URC	15	50			65	/		
SA	Shofar CC	30	10	20		60		/	
N	Mountain Fire Mir.Mins.		50			50		/	
Co	New Jerusalem EC		50			50		/	/
G	Highland		40			40		/	
G	Gloryland Mins		40			40		/	
W	Summerstown EC	25	15			40	/		
G	Ghanaian Presb.	40				40		/	/
W	St. Mary's S'town	15	25			40	/		
R	Russian SDA Church	40				40		/	
N	RCCG Living Waters		30			30		/	
Ca	Brethren	10	20			30	/		
Co	Assembly of God Glory		30			30		/	/
SL	S London Tamil Ch.			30		30		/	/
B	Crista Conscienza				30	30		/	/
Ca	God is Gracious Mins.		25			25		/	
B	UCKG				25	25		/	
G	Lighthouse Chapel		25			25		/	
N	RCCG King's Court		20			20		/	
Co	Glory of God EC		20			20		/	/
N	Christ Life Church		20			20		/	
G	Tuokufio London F'ship		20			20		/	
Ca	Barbadian Nurses		20			20		/	
N	Nigerian Nurses		15			15		/	
N	KICC		10			10		/	
G	Raah ICC		10			10		/	
W	Tooting Grace F'ship	10				10	/		
Total 44 chs.		490	2895	330	185	3900	15	29	10
% background		13	74	8	5				

P = predominant people group (number of fellowships):

B = Brazilian (3)
Ca = Caribbean (9)
Co = Congolese (4)
F = Filipino (1)
G = Ghanaian (10)
Ma = Mauritian (1)
N = Nigerian (6)
R =Russian (1)
SA = South African (1)
SL = Sri Lankan (2)
W = White (6)

Tooting has a population of around 65,000 people, maybe 30% Asian, 30% African and African-Caribbean and 40% white, of which maybe three quarters are 54 or under (i.e. post-moderns, if brought up in the West). Asians would be a mixture of Hindus, Muslims, Sikhs and Buddhists with a small number of Christians. White people would be predominantly non-Christian.

3900 evangelical and Pentecostal Christians meet in 44 churches, of whom 74% are Black, 8% Asian, 5% Latin American and 13% white. These figures show some similarity to the current proportions of peoples in the world church, so I believe they can be instructive in both shedding light on where Christians are at worldwide at present and how progress might be made.

What these figures also show, for evangelical Christians, is that there can be parts of cities in Britain where white Christians can be in an ethnic minority among Christians in that area. With the contraction of the white church, and some growth among African, Asian and Latin American Christians, this may become increasingly common in some areas. When the majority of Christians locally seem to have a quite different way of thinking from yourself, your way of thinking is challenged. There can be different ways to react. One way is to batten down the hatches, to write off other ways of thinking as heretical, and to work with a vision to build a predominantly white church similar to the one that you may have come from, whether in the suburbs or the country. Another response can be to find out as much as possible about how people different from yourself think, evaluate it, and try to understand what God is saying to you through these Christians. I have tried to take the latter approach.

Many of the white Christians living and worshipping in the inner city would be middle class people who have moved in or driven in from the suburbs or from the country, since the majority of the British church is white, middle class. However, the majority of long-term African, Asian, Latin American and white residents in the inner city would be working class. Working class people recognize class differences and oppression, whereas white middle class people find these harder to recognise. Class is another parameter that white middle class Christians in the inner city are relatively blind to the issues around, in addition to race/ethnicity, gender and age/culture.

60 years ago, 11 churches, all with their own premises, comprised most evangelicals in Tooting, most of these being white. Today the white people in those churches are only 8% of all evangelicals and Pentecostals in Tooting. White Christians living in or worshipping in all these churches in Tooting today constitute just under 500 people. At that point people might be talking about a spiritual disaster in the inner city. However, people from Africa, Asia and Latin America have in the last 60 years increased that number of evangelicals by over 700%!

One sad aspect of this is that while the balance of evangelicals and Pentecostals in the last 60 years in Tooting has shifted from predominantly white to predominantly African, Asian and Latin American there has appeared to be little if any change in the culture of the traditional denominations, regardless of how several have become Black Majority Churches (defined as a church where over half the people are of African, Asian or Latin American origin). However one looks at things, two points are clear. First, traditional denominations appear to have made it clear that any Christians from other ethnic groups who wish to join their church must do things the same way as those white people do them or go somewhere else. However, in a survey that I carried out in one traditional denomination church that is also a Black Majority Church, the most important issue to the membership was an acceptance and welcome as equals to people of all backgrounds in the church and the community. Second, in Tooting 79% of all evangelicals and Pentecostals are now outside the traditional denominations' church buildings and do not have a building of their own. This causes tremendous problems when those evangelicals and Pentecostals without their own buildings seek to buy their own premises. Secular authorities really struggle with this: the view is that Christian churches already have perhaps too many premises of their own. The white response from within the traditional denominations of 'Come and join us!' does not address long-standing issues of white domination, control and racism that are considered below.

Today, four church buildings formerly owned by traditional denominations or predominantly white Christian organizations are now owned by African-Caribbean churches. In each case, it was only a financial crisis, the inability of the traditional denomination or organization to operate the premises profitably, that had caused the predominantly white Christian group to sell to African-Caribbeans, that is, to make a crisis decision. This is a further pointer that many relationships between traditional denominations and African, Asian and Latin American churches and Christians are economic, rather than relationships of equals and partnerships. I believe it also shows that it is not until white evangelicals are in crisis that they will consider giving up their own control to African and Asian peoples.

I look now to develop further this comparison by comparing the characteristics of white and Majority World evangelicalism and Pentecostalism in UK in order to develop some conclusions that might also have some relevance for other forms of Christianity in UK.

Characteristics of present-day British evangelical Christianity
Evangelicalism, which began in the eighteenth century as a network of movements in Britain and her colonies, developed from three streams: first, post-1660 pietism (Bunyan, Doddridge, Watts); second the Moravians; third, Anglican high church spirituality (the 'Holy Club'). Evangelicalism has the following consistent pattern of convictions:
. Biblicism (reliance on Bible as authority);

. Conversionism (new birth);
. Activism (individual, energetic involvement in religious duties and social action);
. Crucicentrism (the cross as the centre of Christian faith) (Noll, 2003; Bebbington, 1989).

Richard Turnbull (2006), in a videoed presentation to the 2006 Reform conference, characterizes British evangelicals as being people concerned for four things:
. the inerrancy of scripture;
. the penal substitution of the cross;
. a personal relationship with God through Christ;
. sharing faith in evangelism.

Some people have problems with this latter statement of evangelicalism, for example:
. Christian hope is presented as 'Going to heaven when we die'. As an alternative others have seen that in the resurrection of Jesus God is starting to remake the world through the church, meaning that there is a lot more for the church to do on earth in addition to evangelism (Wright, 2011).
. Greek dualism causes people to see the spiritual as good and the material as bad. While the focus on evangelism may be seen as good it ignores injustice for the majority of people. How can I say that 'Jesus Christ makes you free' (John 8. 32) to a Pakistani Muslim if white working class men on average receive 150 pounds per week, or 7,500 pounds each year, more than Pakistani working class men in UK?
. Church is often an oppressive institution. One area of oppression is where white middle class men control what happens rather than leaving control to the Spirit. In practice there is little space in traditional conservative white evangelicalism for the Holy Spirit, beyond the Spirit's work in regeneration and sanctification. The more 'supernatural' gifts of the Spirit (e.g. miracles, speaking in tongues, words of revelation, prophecy) are understood by conservatives to have ceased in spite of all that the New Testament says about them. The penalty of believing they have ceased (often not explained to the church) is that the first five books of the New Testament are today seen by cessationists to have no relevance to Christians today beyond being 'The History of Salvation', that is, the story of the incarnation, death and resurrection of Christ and the giving of the Spirit at Pentecost (Gaffin, 1996).
. Conservative evangelicalism appears to have little space for postmodern expressions of spirituality.

Two other types of evangelical are open and charismatic. Graham Kings (2003) defines these within the Anglican Church. For Kings, open evangelicals are committed to:
. the trustworthiness and authority of the Bible (which is interpreted in context and with the world church's insights)

. the longing for conversion to Christ of everyone (from all faiths and none)
. working for renewal within Anglicanism
   and are open to
. the Holy Spirit's work
. learning from other Anglican traditions
. working with churches from other denominations
. fruits of biblical scholarship
. issues of justice
. significance of the sacraments
. learning from people of other faiths
. ordination of women
   He views charismatic evangelicals as committed to
. trustworthiness and dynamic authority of the Bible (listening to the Spirit)
. mission in the power of the Spirit (including signs and wonders)
. exercising spiritual gifts (including healing, prophecy and tongues)
   and open to:
. sharing celebrations with other denominations
. the ministry of women
. working with possession and oppression by evil spirits
. the importance of communal aspects of church
. worldwide charismatic and pentecostal movements.
   In terms of size and trends, the following is the UK situation for evangelicals:

Table 5
Evangelicals in England (Brierley, 2013 and 2014)

	1998	Change	2005	Change	2012
Open	217900	-20%	175500	N/A	N/A
Conservative	645500	-10%	584700	N/A	N/A
Charismatic	527900	-5%	504600	N/A	N/A
Total	1391300	-9%	1264800	N/A	N/A

of whom
Evangelicals in Greater London

	1998	Change	2005	Change	2012
Open	17900	-9%	16300	-5%	15500
Conservative	126700	+9%	137700	+24%	170800
Charismatic	121200	+12%	135300	+41%	191000
Total	265800	+9%	289300	+30%	377300

The growth in Charismatic Evangelicals in Greater London results primarily from the growth of Black Majority Churches.

Characteristics of evangelical Christianity in the Majority World
In order to identify the characteristics of the evangelical and renewalist Christianity that has been growing since 1960 in the Majority World, and in view of the difficulty in getting representative data on evangelicals today, I turn to *Spirit and Power: A 10-Country Survey of Pentecostals* (2006). Countries surveyed are Brazil, Chile, Guatemala, India, Nigeria, Philippines, South Africa, South Korea and the United States. The *World Christian Database* says that Pentecostals and Charismatics now comprise one-quarter of all 'Christians' or 500 million people worldwide, second only to Roman Catholics in number of adherents. In Latin America, Pentecostals are now three-quarters of all Protestants. Pentecostals are members either of traditional Pentecostal denominations or of independent indigenous churches, while Charismatics are members of traditionally non-Pentecostal denominations, including, for example, Anglican, Orthodox or Roman Catholic denominations. In general, if a person is Pentecostal they will also be evangelical. If a person indicates they are Charismatic they may or may not be evangelical.

Table 6 Pentecostals and Charismatics as a proportion of Protestants

	% of Protestants who are		
	Pente-Costals	Charis-matics	Non-renewalists
United States	10	18	72
Latin America			
Brazil	72	6	22
Chile	59	19	22
Guatemala	58	27	15
Africa			
Kenya	50	23	27
Nigeria	48	12	40
South Africa	14	29	57
Asia			
India*	N/A	N/A	N/A
Philippines	37	30	33
South Korea	9	29	62

* India sample size of Protestants too small

Characteristics of Majority World Pentecostals and Charismatics, in comparison with those of non-renewalist (i.e. not Pentecostal or Charismatic) Christians as researched by the American team include:
. scriptures to be taken literally (over 70% of Pentecostals except Philippines);
. duty to evangelise (64% or more of Pentecostals);
. faith shared with non-believers once a week (over 50% of Pentecostals, except Nigeria and India);
. church services frequently include gifts of the Spirit, such as tongues, praying for healing, prophesying (over half Pentecostals in 7 of 10 countries). N.B. in 6 of the 10 countries, 40% of Pentecostals say they never speak or pray in tongues;
. personally experienced or witnessed divine healing of an injury or illness (56%-87% of Pentecostals in all countries);
. personally experienced or witnessed exorcism (50% or more of Pentecostals in 7 of 10 countries);
. religious groups should express their views on social and political questions (50% or more of Pentecostals in all countries except India);
. work for justice for the poor (84% or more of Pentecostals in all countries);
' drinking alcohol can never be justified (50% or more of Pentecostals in all countries except U.S.);
. divorce can never be justified (50% or more of Pentecostals in 6 of 10 countries);
. women allowed to serve as pastors or church leaders (50% or more of Pentecostals in 6 of 10 countries) (Spirit and Power, 2006).
    If I may add characteristics that I have observed among Majority World origin Christians in Tooting I would add
. tremendous faith in liberation from oppression in this life, expressed through
. fasting at least once a week, including perhaps fasting for a month; and through
. believing prayer. Many Tooting churches have all-night or half-night prayer at least once a month. I've noticed generally that while white people usually pray for things that cause the system of oppression to stay in place, Black and Asian people usually pray so that they would get liberation from white people's oppression;
. the ability to interpret and preach the Bible under the Spirit's activity in such a way as to cause people who are 'dry bones' to be resurrected each week;
. the ability not only to keep their faith but also to provide pastoral comfort and help to their community in the face of continuous discrimination and injustice.

The Ecumenical Movement - an opportunity missed
The original impetus for ecumenism, working together with other Christians, came from African, Asian and Latin American Christians (Philip, 1999). This was at a time that the comity of mission societies was stopping those African, Asian and Latin American Christians from coming together with each other and with the churches of

the West. Comity was the forming of agreements between Western mission societies dividing up the country between them so that there was no competition between mission societies, and hence between denominations, within any one area.

From the perspective of white evangelical Christians, who were perhaps the dominant group in Protestant mission societies, the power in the Ecumenical Movement came to be held by white liberals. White evangelicals had struggled already in Western denominations in the face of liberal power and tended to look at the Ecumenical Movement through the lenses of their local context of ecumenism where many evangelicals saw themselves as oppressed minorities in predominantly liberal denominations in the West.

White evangelicals also believed the Ecumenical Movement maximized its focus on improving life in this world while minimizing a focus on conversion that looked to the next world. The modern dualism of Western white evangelicals caused them to see salvation of the soul as good and work to bring liberation to oppressed people in this life as bad. It also caused them to believe in the all importance of right thinking on Biblical doctrine, and about the need to have power over other people, whether white liberals or African, Asian or Latin American Christians. Ecumenism, as a result, became another subject to be demonized by modern white evangelicals.

The Ecumenical Movement did give an opportunity for dialogue and listening to the concerns of African, Asian and Latin American Christians. This opportunity was greater than that in the context of mission agencies, where the focus was more on monologue and getting the evangelistic message out. However, the concerns for righting the wrongs in this world that were the just grievances of Majority World Christians became largely associated in the minds of Western evangelicals with the views of Western liberals that they were struggling against because of their conviction that evangelism was the pre-eminent message, causing evangelicals to focus on the next world at the expense of focusing on this world. Western evangelicals' overwhelming need to maintain control in order to convey their view of the primacy of evangelism resulted in a continued unwillingness to listen to the just grievances of Majority World Christians and the demonizing of a major place for listening to the concerns of Majority World Christians.

How to understand differences between evangelicals/Pentecostals that are African, Asian, Latin American and white

Some of these convictions of Black, Asian and Latin American evangelicals (e.g. scriptural reliability, evangelism) are similar to traditional British conservative evangelicalism, while others (e.g. gifts of the Spirit, fasting) seem considerably different. Can people have fellowship together or is this heresy? Is there some way of understanding why one person understands Jesus in a different way from another? Or, as Jacques Derrida (1976) maintains, how a different community has a different interpretation?

. The effect of dualistic religious ground motives on thinking in the West
Herman Dooyeweerd, a forerunner of today's leading philosophers, shows that at any given moment Western people's thinking is driven by one of four ground motives, or worldviews, that have governed Western thought over the last 2,500 years. Dooyeweerd's work has been presented in a more popular apologetic way by Francis Schaeffer (1972, 1998 and 2007). We have to remember that Schaeffer and Dooyeweerd argue from a modern viewpoint. Their views might therefore need to be understood in a slightly different way for engaging with postmoderns.   The four ground motives are:
. MFGM – Matter-Form motive from ancient Greece (dualism);
. CFR – Creation-Fall-Redemption motive from the Hebrews (integrative);
. NGGM – Nature-Grace motive from Roman Catholicism in the Middle Ages (dualism);
. NFGM – Nature-Freedom motive from Renaissance, Enlightenment and Modern sources (dualism) (Dooyeweerd, 1980 and 2003; Choi, 2006).

Dooyeweerd says that everyone has an underlying religious presupposition about what is self-dependent and Divine. This underlies our ground motives or presuppositions about reality and good and evil. These develop into worldviews of how we think about life, from which we develop theories to guide our living.

What happens is that people tend to switch between different ground motives, so Christians who may try to follow the Creation-Fall-Redemption motive may well switch to operating according to a different ground motive in the space of a few seconds. When we at any moment follow one of these three dualistic ground motives and, for example, choose the Divine, we reject other parts of creation that we see as 'evil' (e.g. the material creation, everyday work life) and are therefore rejecting various aspects of life that God has made. Alternatively, we can follow the non-divine way, which indicates that there are ways we can do our lives that do not need to follow what God says in the Bible (so we follow our reason rather than our faith).

Through Western Christians following these three dualisms and failing to effectively challenge the claims of reason, and then science and secularism to explain God and life, a number of bad results have happened. First, a generation of evangelicals in the West has given birth to generations of secularists (this has happened more slowly in the U.S. than in Europe). Second, many Western Christians privatize their faith and effectively live the public aspect of their lives according to secularist principles, which is noticed by non-Christians. This makes it difficult for them to challenge injustice in the world and their witness to people of other cultures as a result of this has few favourable results. Third, Black and Asian people see the hypocrisy of Western Christians because their own worldviews are integral, i.e. the personal, social, economic, political and faith aspects of their lives are all consistent with each other.

The evangelicalism of the West therefore distorts the faith of the New Testament. This distortion reflects secularism among Western evangelicals; it includes a disbelief in the spirit world owing to rationalism; the understanding of evangelical faith in the terms of modernism; a dualism that prioritises the spiritual at the expense of the secular (unless it's one's own family's security); and lifestyles that give out a message that white people are superior to Black, Asian and Latin American peoples.

. The nature of the cultures into which the Gospel has been, or has yet to be contextualized

Michael Cooper (2003) quotes Alister McGrath (1995) as saying that in the West evangelical identity has been based upon the Reformation. Western evangelical identity has as a result become tied to modernity and modernity is seen as irrelevant by postmoderns and by Black, Asian and Latin American people. Cooper says that Kwame Bediako looks at how Western Christianity engaged with Greek thought and also considers how African identity might be understood, both in terms of Western Christianity and in terms of African Traditional Religions.

Bediako (1999) shows that when Christianity was contextualized by early church Greek fathers such as Justin Martyr and Clement of Alexandria in order to show the validity of a Christian identity for Graeco-Romans, they pointed to precursors of Christian faith among people following the philosophical 'Form' religion of Socrates. This was fine since the emphasis was on the superiority of the Christian revelation. However, there was a subsequent introduction of Middle Platonism and Neo-Platonism into the Latin Church in the Dark Ages, and also the rise of the Scholastic movement and the attempt by Thomas Aquinas to merge the thought of Aristotle with the Bible in *Summa Theologica* that is still the theological basis of the Roman Catholic Church (Schaff, 1960).

Bediako shows that Bolaji Idowu (1962) and John Mbiti (1969, 1970 and 1975b) were two theologians that found that in order to understand African Christian identity and in order to contextualize Christianity for Africans we need to look at African Traditional Religions. These show the prior operation of God in African societies before the 'third opportunity', the bringing of the Gospel to Africa by Western Protestant missionaries. In his trilogy, Mbiti shows that at root African Religions are monotheistic and that African people's prayers show their preparedness for the Gospel. Bediako identifies that primal religions underlie the Christian faith of the majority of the world's Christians. Central to these primal religions is the interdependence and interrelationships between all creation – God, the spirit world including ancestors, humans, animals, plants, animate and inanimate creation (Turner, 1977). People have regular experiences, for example, of engaging with people who are demon-possessed, praying for healing when there are no drugs available, even dealing with situations where people have died and they are called on to raise the dead. In a traditional denomination church in Tooting I heard a testimony from one church leader who confessed to two occasions on which he was instrumental in bringing back people from the dead. As such, this involvement with the spirit world means that involvement with the gifts of the Spirit will be crucial to these Christians' faith.

Some people might respond with the concern, 'But this looks like what has happened is syncretism'. Syncretism, or the mixing of non-Christian religion with Christianity, was one of the major fears of Western missionaries. Fear of syncretism contributed to the lack of effort that people made to contextualize. We do not have the space to consider this fully. However, to respond briefly, Mack Harling (2005) notes that this fear of syncretism was exactly the fear of the Judaizers in the New Testament, whose view was dismissed in favour of sensitivity to the cultural concerns of Gentile Christians. Therefore, the response of the Jerusalem council in Acts 15 showed that people from a non-Christianity-based religio-socio-cultural background should be allowed to follow Christ without forsaking their own heritage.

Following Bediako's analysis, Geoff Holsclaw (2004) looks at how Bediako's work has relevance for people with a postmodern identity. Christianity is therefore being worked out worldwide in different cultural contexts with specific cultural expressions of the faith handed down. Cooper says people need to identify a model of Christianity through which they can engage with ethnic identity, not so as to conform those different identities to a set of doctrines, but through the diversity of people to understand more about all people's relationships with God.

In practice, three factors conspired in Europe to wipe a belief in the Spirit's gifts out of the European worldview: the joining of church and state under Constantine that imposed the state form of religion and brought an end to Mediterranean primal religions; unbelief and a desire to control; and the conspiring of reason, science and secularism to declare that what could not be seen did not exist. In African, Asian and Latin American worldviews, however, both God and the spirit world were integrally involved with people in daily decision-making, so involvement with the gifts of the Spirit came far more naturally to Christians from these backgrounds. Elsewhere, Cooper (2005) says people need to look at history to see the way that the neo-colonialist culture of US (and Britain) has distorted Western Christianity and caused it to be rejected by postmoderns, and by Black and Asian people.

Evangelicals shrinking in number in England
Figures in Table 5 show that evangelicals are falling in numbers in England, comprising 2.5% of the English population in 2005. Having said that, numbers of

Black, Asian and Latin American evangelicals are growing and currently are at one-quarter of all evangelicals in England. 23% of all evangelicals in England were in Greater London in 2005, a proportion forecast to grow to 29% by 2015. One encouragement was that 'Emerging Churches' totaled 18,000 people in 2005, with an average age of 29 (average age nationally of all churchgoers was 45).

With the numbers of people leaving the churches, particularly the numbers of young people, it is crucial to be finding out the thoughts of the 40% of people who have left churches and to understand the spirituality of postmoderns. Showing and sharing the Christian faith needs to happen in a different way from in the past because people from such a wide range of backgrounds have given up on traditional churches, even evangelical churches, that use old approaches.

Dar-es-Salaam – a possible pointer to future Global North/South encounters
Jesus tells the story of the Good Samaritan (Luke 10. 29-37) not long after James and John had threatened to burn up a Samaritan village (Luke 9. 54). In the parable Jesus shows that people need to learn how to be a neighbour from the example of the Samaritan, that is, from a people whose guts they themselves may hate. In the same way that Jesus had a ministry in and through the Samaritans, I believe Jesus has a ministry both in and through Majority World Christian people today that may shame some attitudes of white Christians.

An example that shows the serial retreat and advance of Christianity mentioned by Lamin Sanneh above was the Anglican Primates meeting in Dar-es-Salaam, Tanzania, February 14th-19th, 2007. The Anglican Communion is the third largest Christian denomination in the world with 48 million members. Africa alone has 32 million members. Nigeria, with 11.3 million members, has more members than England (2.8 million), Australia (3.8 million), Canada (0.7 million), New Zealand (0.6 million) and the United States (2.4 million) combined (10.3 million). The presenting issue at the conference was The Episcopal Church's (TEC - United States) response to the communiqué at the previous primates meeting (Dromantine, Northern Ireland, 2005) that they cease blessing same-sex unions (SSUs). This presenting issue was one aspect of a more general move in TEC towards universalism.

At the end of the day, the meeting came down to a contest between white, liberal control and growing African and Asian 'conservative' power. Interestingly, white American TEC conservatives see themselves as having been discriminated against by liberals for the last 40 years without any power to do anything about it (Hey, 2007). Similar comments have been made about the situation in England. Henry Orombi admits that it was the hardest meeting he had ever been in. But the communiqué and schedule released after working through the night appeared to give almost all that Majority World and American conservatives wanted, with unanimous approval by the primates (Global South Anglican website).

There are some useful pointers from this meeting. The communiqué together with the Covenant issued is probably the first written example of communion-wide discipline in the five hundred year history of the Anglican Communion. Also, the top priority of the Archbishop of Canterbury (ABC) appeared to be to maintain unity in the face of possible schism by putting off indefinitely discipline of TEC. It appears that this continued unity is for the purpose of developing closer ties with the Roman Catholic Church, which has a worldwide communion, although its management style is quite different from the Anglican model. This policy was clearly overcome at Dar-es-Salaam. To avoid schism long-term the last thing one might want to do is to threaten one party with removal from the communion if they do not change their behaviour within eight months.

Further, and perhaps one reason for the content of the communiqué was the ABC, Rowan Williams' cultural background and style. Being a Western modern, Williams sought to use a Hegelian dialectic in order to reach unity. He took the thesis of a liberal TEC which spoke of social justice before biblical content, added to it the antithesis of the global South that gave a conservative Bible reading and looked for a synthesis to find a way forward. But the world situation is different now from before. The majority of Anglicans are now in the Global South and apparently between 16 and 21 of the 38 Anglican provinces worldwide wanted a conservative solution. Conservatives refused to put up with opposition by liberals. In order to get a unanimous communiqué most of the expectations of the conservatives had to be met.

Again, one trump card that Global South primates were able to play related to their worldview compared with the European worldview. Because white people are dualistic, white liberals focused only on justice issues, treating evangelical arguments for evangelism of 'the Other' as misguided. Global South primates focused both on justice and on truth and evangelism etc., because their worldview is holistic. Their arguments therefore outflanked white liberal arguments.

Finally, Philip Jenkins (2007) has indicated that other traditional denominations might well see a similar confrontation between majority conservative churches in the Global South and minority predominantly liberal churches in the West.

Conclusions

The growth in faith among Majority World peoples has resulted in very little change in the attitude of white people towards Black and Asian people. White people's approach is generally still one of white supremacy. Examples of respect and appreciation by white people for Black and Asian people are rare. One exception is regular messages on the *Stand Firm* blog. It seems that the experience of evangelicals in The Episcopal Church of the USA has been so deeply troubling that after 40 years of struggle with modernists they are grateful to run into the arms of Global South primates who are organizing alternative primatial oversight (APO) for orthodox congregations in the United States. It will be interesting to see whether white people's involvement with, for example, Africans in Africa might lead to an improved relationship between white people and African-Americans.

Also, Black, Asian and Latin American Christians predominantly came to faith through national evangelists rather than through white missionaries since nationals were able to contextualize their faith in their home countries, whereas white missionaries were not able to contextualize their faith in these other countries. White assumptions of the validity of modern culture will not work in the West now. No more modern people are being born, only postmoderns. Note also that the average age of evangelicals in England is now below 45: people of all ages up to 54 brought up in the West are postmodern. It is time for the church in England to change or die.

Further, Lamin Sanneh (2003) speaks of two streams moving in opposite directions: secularism in the West filling the void from which faith has been drained is moving from the West to the Majority World, while the growth in the Majority World of Christianity as a world religion is moving with migrants to the West. Could the shrinkage of evangelicals in Europe result also from becoming part of the global rich? Are the global rich willing to give back to the poor, or at least learn from them?

Finally, the Dar-es-Salaam Primates meeting was a warning of a changing Christian world. But this is not only a warning to liberals who might downplay the Bible but also to white evangelicals seeking to impose their version of modern Western evangelicalism on Black, Asian and Latin American Christians. Theologians in the Majority World have other priorities than those in the West, as the Global South Anglican website makes clear.

Chapter 3
The Western Christian missionary movement until independence

'At last the end of an old era! ... This celebration will in fact be a manifesto of liberation from the missions largely shaped, conditioned and largely carried out by the churches in the West. How can the church in the Third World preach the gospel of liberation when she is fettered in the traditions and practices of Western Christian missions? When she is considered as a part and parcel of Western religious and cultural phenomena? Hence, if she is still haunted by the apparition of Western foreign missions, let us drive it away with firecrackers. If she is still afraid of the ghost of the Western missionary past, let us scare it away with beating of drums and of cymbals.... For a new era of Christian mission, a Copernican revolution of ideas and practices related to mission is necessary' (Choan-Seng Song, 1977).

'Jesus' parables (tell) the Israel-story in order to undermine the present way of understanding the nation's identity. It is as though someone were to tell the story of America, or of the British Empire, not, as the Americans and British normally tell them, as the stories of freedom and civilization and how they were achieved, but as stories of Promethean ambition achieving deeply ambiguous power, handling it with irresponsible self-righteousness, and facing imminent disaster as a result' (Wright, 1996).

Here I consider first work in Africa. Bible translation was perhaps the most important Western contribution, helping Africans to contextualize their faith for Africans, which white people couldn't do. In India, many missionaries saw Indian society as inferior to British society. This and their working closely with colonial administrators set back Indians from turning to faith in Christ until after independence.

To the extent to which white Christian people think of Black and Asian people at all *consciously* they might view them as targets or objects for evangelism. People from 10/40 window country backgrounds, including asylum seekers, who may be seen to be from unreached people groups, may be attractive to people for evangelistic purposes. Social projects, e.g. English language teaching or food distribution, may be undertaken but only as a means of building relationships in order to share the Gospel. Having said this, Christians from Black and Asian backgrounds in church are assumed to think the same way as white Christians, expected to be seen and not heard and to conform in their behaviour to how things have been done in the past in that church. Having Black and Asian Christians in one's congregation is primarily a sign that your ministry has an appeal beyond the white, middle class.

The thinking that is at work here might include the following:

. Greek dualism, absorbed early into European Christianity, that effectively treats the spiritual as good and the material as bad. It focuses on spiritual (a vertical relationship with God) and otherworldly aims including that people are seen as objects that need their souls saving from eternal death. By implication, it sees horizontal relationship with one's human neighbour as an equal and concern for their material wellbeing in this life as secondary, if not insignificant;

. Treating people as objects to be evangelized is part of a wider activity that tends to dominate people and keep them subordinate;

. Assumptions about how Black and Asian people think can owe more to ignorance and depend on how white people view them, resulting in stereotyping all people from an ethnic background according to how one person from that background may have been perceived to act.

Having thought about how white non-Christian and Christian people might view Black and Asian people, we are now in a position to compare this personal research and reflection on how white non-Christian and Christian people actually engaged with Black and Asian people in history in the home countries of Black and Asian people. For the colonial background, see *CG*, ch. 1.

Protestant Christian mission in Africa

White evangelical Christian missionaries have had consistent views over the last several hundred years. The top priority in this life is to share your faith so that someone else comes to faith in Christ and therefore can go to heaven in the next life. Any social activity is only justifiable to the extent that it enables you to share your faith with other people. The focus on the next life at the expense of involvement in the present life may be accepted by others when there are comparatively few social problems for the majority but there may be problems when the majority's socio-economic experience is of substantial social injustice. Views on faith and practice are held to as 'absolute truth' by many modern white Christians, rather than in any way being shaped or distorted by Western thinking or culture. It is assumed that the traditional daily life of Christians in Britain meets God's requirements and little reflection is given as to how this might be viewed by people from different cultures (e.g. Winter, Hawthorne et al. 1999; Johnstone 1998; McGavran 1970).

In the opinion of Lamin Sanneh, white people's greatest gift to Africa in terms of the Christian message was working with Africans to translate the Bible into local, vernacular languages. An example that Kwame Bediako gives of translation work is the work pioneered by Johannes Christaller of the Basel Mission, together with his African colleagues, Jonathan Bekoe Palmer and David Asante, at Akropong in the

Gold Coast, modern day Ghana. By the 1850s, the Basel Mission was running infant, primary and middle schools, together with the Theological Seminary, started in 1848. Christaller's purpose was to form 'Christian nations'. Emphasising national histories he said, 'A nation is on the path to civilization when it tries to recollect its own history, when it begins to compare its former and present state, to disapprove and reject bad observances, and to rejoice in real improvements, to learn from the past, and to progress towards what is better... and so I hope that Ga and Twi Christians also in future days will be glad to read about the conditions and transactions of their ancestors' (Jenkins, 1973). For Sanneh (1990, 1993), translation of the Bible into local languages, including adopting local names for God into the translation, not only enabled Africans to develop their own cultural materials using their local language, but also showed them a message about the impartiality of God with respect to people of all ethnic backgrounds that enabled true Christianity to become a front for the growth of resistance to the colonialism of the foreigners.

The ministry of Christian missionaries was problematic to Africans. Owing to the lack of effective Christian challenging of secularism in the West, Western Christians embodied a secularist lifestyle (Noll, 1994). This manifested itself in the missionaries' focus on sharing their faith, but leaving the colonial administration to set the standards with respect to economics, politics, social and personal life. As Africans were holistic – for them faith, politics, economic, social and personal life were all one – they saw through the hypocrisy of the missionary. The force of secularism was such that the inescapable conclusion was that the white distortion of Christianity was one which was just another arm of control and manipulation by the secularist colonial administration. However, the message that Africans received from the translated Bible was one that showed that the Christian faith is indeed holistic and therefore highly relevant to the African worldview. This provided the basis for Africanisation of the Christian faith, initially by African Independent Churches, from the late nineteenth century onwards.

When missionaries went to Africa they did so with a mission agency. If the mission agency was a denominational one, a denominational church was started: Anglican, Presbyterian, Methodist, Baptist, Assemblies of God, etc. Most of these denominations and more are now seen locally in Tooting, South London as separate expressions of church by, for example, Ghanaian people (e.g. Ghanaian Presbyterian, Baptist, Methodist, Assemblies of God, Elim and Seventh Day Adventist churches in Tooting). In terms of moving towards unity, the white mission agencies' response in Africa was to agree for each mission to have sovereignty over a geographical area, which other mission agencies agreed not to intrude into. This practice was known as 'comity'. While this might have looked like unity from the mission agencies' viewpoint, local people found that in practice they were not allowed to go to another denomination if they disagreed with the denomination in their area. This, together with Africanisation mentioned above, was to fuel the increase in people leaving traditional denominations to join African independent and pentecostal churches. The main impetus for Christian unity in Africa and Asia came from national churches which felt frustrated by missionary denominationalism and paternalism (Philip, 1999).

Ngugi Wa Thiong'O (1986) says that acceptance of the church meant rejecting all values and rituals that kept people together and adopting European middle class behaviour. 'In Kenya, while the European settler robbed people of their land and the products of their sweat, the missionary robbed people of their soul. Thus was the African body and soul bartered for thirty pieces of silver and the promise of a European heaven'.

Vincent Donovan (2006), a Roman Catholic priest, went to work among the Masai in Kenya in 1965. Looking back over 100 years of Roman Catholic mission in East Africa, he saw that the first approach of the Catholic church in East Africa, buying and baptizing slaves, had not worked. The second approach, building schools and training up children as Catholics, had resulted in an inward-looking, individualistic, salvation-oriented, and unadapted Christianity being planted in Africa. A third approach, giving aid and material help without any strings attached following independence, seemed to be devoid of Christian content. In response, Donovan had to develop a pioneer, contextualized, evangelistic approach using virtually no resources except asking the Maasai themselves.

Kwame Bediako (1983) usefully summarises the impact of missionary work on Africa. Bediako quotes Adrian Hastings (1967) saying that missionaries were struck by the awfulness of Africa, that anything pre-Christian was seen as valueless. Bediako feels that the reasons for this were threefold. First, relationships with Africans were overshadowed by 400 years of enslavement. In 1772 when slavery was ruled illegal in England, the only person to have served as an Anglican clergyman in West Africa wrote a pamphlet in which he justified the slave trade based on Aristotle's ideas and scripture (Thompson, 1772). Secondly, racist ideas in Europe had made Africans bottom of the racial hierarchy. William Carey's views (1792) were typical of many when he said of Africans that they were, 'as destitute of civilization as they are of true religion'. Thirdly, that white people both identified 'Christianity' with 'European' and with 'civilization'. For an African-American view of white American missionary work in South Africa, see Daryl Balia (2007).

How missionaries viewed the African world is shown in the proceedings of the Edinburgh conference in 1910. E. B. Tylor had classified the religion of 'primitive' peoples as 'animism'. W. H. T. Gairdner (1910) understood this to be 'the religious beliefs of more or less backward and degraded peoples all over the world'. When comparing this system with other religious systems – Chinese religions, religions of Japan, Islam and Hinduism – Gairdner said of 'animism' that it was 'surely the humblest of all possible teachers... and the least sublime of all the five creeds'. At

52

the Le Zoute conference in 1929 Africans were treated with a bit more respect: Dietrich Westermann (1926) said, 'The Africans have been treated by us as having no religion, no language, no tradition, no institutions, no racial character of their own, as empty vessels to be filled with European and American goods'. And yet in the Duff Lectures in 1935, Westermann (1937) was urging missionaries to be ruthless in rooting out African Traditional Religions.

In answering the question why a genuine encounter between the Gospel and African religious life did not take place, Bediako first refers to Roland Allen's writings earlier in the twentieth century. Allen (1978 and 1979) indicated how western missionaries were hindering the growth of emergent churches. The cultural assumptions that surrounded church planting amounted to a 'Judaizing' activity, whereby missionaries tended to preach the Law in the guise of a Europeanized Gospel as if it was pure Gospel. Effectively, as G.C. Oosthuizen (1968) says, the missionaries were saying that Africans must become like the missionaries. Oosthuizen identifies well that Africa had no Paul. This means that no-one found out what the worldviews of Africans were, what the Christian faith might look like shorn of the white worldview and enculturated in an African worldview, what Africans' questions might be of that faith, and how that faith could be contextualized in a way that Africans might understand. It might be instructive to ask what might have become of faith today if the 'Judaizers' had won the day in New Testament times.

Andrew Walls (1970) helpfully shows that the missionaries who viewed Africans as 'heathens' were distorting Romans 1. Somehow world religions slipped into the place of 'ungodly men', while Christianity took the place of 'the righteousness of God'. This judgmental approach is itself judged by seeing that in Romans 3 Paul says that *all* people have sinned. Paul's achievement was in transposing the Gospel from the Jewish world into the Hellenistic world, always understanding that the fullness of that work would need to be completed by Hellenistic Christians.

The reason that this type of facilitating work of Paul was not done in Africa is shown by S. G. Williamson (1965). Williamson says of missionaries' encounter with Akan people in Ghana, that missionaries denied the Akan world-view on the ground of a white world-view. The Akan became a Christian by doing things as the missionary said and being drawn away from their traditional life, rather than by working out their salvation in Christ within their traditional religious way of thinking. John Mbiti (1969) has confirmed that Williamson's view was similar to the situation in other African countries. John V. Taylor sees this activity by white people in terms of Christ being presented in answer to the questions European men ask, rather than in answer to the questions Africans ask.

By way of comparison, Bediako elsewhere looks at missionary work by Africans. The first local church arrived ready-made in the form of African-Americans and African-Canadians repatriated to Sierra Leone following the War of Independence in 1792. Philip Quaque, the first African ordained an Anglican, preached in Gold Coast from 1766 for nine years and 52 people were converted.

By contrast, William Wade Harris (1865-1929) was the first of many Independent African Christian prophets. Harris is an example of an African who not only had a primal understanding of the Gospel but also was self-consciously an African Christian and outside of European missionary finance and control. Through two years of Harris' ministry in Liberia, 120,000 Africans repented of their sins, became Christian believers and were baptized (Howard, 1989; Bediako, 2004; Shank, 1986). Andrew Walls (1989) admits that the growth of Christianity in Africa in the 20th century was to an unexpected extent a result of initiatives by Africans.

Protestant Christian Mission in India

Although Christianity first came to India perhaps through the Apostle Thomas in the founding of the Mar Thoma church in South India, Jacob Dharmaraj says that the first white presence came through Portuguese Catholics, who received large areas of responsibility in south and east Asia from Pope Leo X in 1514. In Goa, Jesuits influenced Governor Barreto to pass laws favouring Christians. By the early seventeenth century, the 20,000 Hindus in Goa were a minority and Christians a majority among a total Goan population of 150,000. Of Portuguese mission in the north, Sisir Kumar Das says, 'The stories of Portuguese savagery haunted the memory of the Bengalis for several centuries and in our own time the novelists exploited these themes with much power and feeling. The conversion of Bengalis into Christianity not only coincided with the activities of the Portuguese pirates in Bengal, but the pirates took an active interest in it. The Bengalis who accepted Christianity were forced to abandon their faith at the point of the sword or they were allured by money' (Philip, 1987).

While the first evangelical Protestant missionaries in India were two Germans, Ziegenbalg and Plutschau, sent to the Danish trading post at Tranquebar in South India in 1706, perhaps the most well-known early British missionary was William Carey, who arrived in Bengal in November 1793. After his money and goods were mismanaged by a fellow-worker, Thomas, an old friend, George Udny, offered Carey and Thomas jobs managing two new indigo factories in North Bengal. The plantation job helped Carey get close to the workers which helped him learn Bengali and Sanskrit. The workers depended on Carey owing to their poverty and this gave him positional advantage to use them as his congregation. Carey received two hundred rupees a month, commission on indigo sold and shares in the works, while local workers were paid four rupees a month or less. So, while white planters considered the people as material used for profit, Carey appears to have treated them as uncivilized pagans fit to be converted.

After the factories were flooded out in 1799, Carey came to Serampore, another Danish colony, and started the Mission. However, he was soon appointed by Lord

Wellesley to teach Bengali on five hundred rupees a month, and then professor of Bengali and Sanskrit at Fort William College in Calcutta, training government administrators, on a thousand rupees a month (although he gave 90% of this to Serampore Mission). In 1813 people in the Molucca Islands asked Lord Moira (later Governor-General Lord Hastings) for Serampore Mission to establish an extension school. Moira promised assistance, visiting Serampore in 1815 and placing orders for a lot of copies of Sanskrit literature. When William Ward spoke in London in 1821 to the Wesleyan Missionary Society he said, 'The Government of India acts, as far as is prudent, entirely with us; and in a variety of ways, they are assisting us, and assisting us in the most powerful manner' (The Missionary Register, 1821).

As people like Ruth and Vishal Mangalwadi (1999), Franklyn J. Balasundaram (2001) and Paul Pease (2005) show, Carey certainly contributed much towards skills development in India. He had lofty ideals shown in delivering innocent victims of Sati and child sacrifice from Hindu religious practices. However, he failed to speak against white oppression. He wrote that all non-Western societies were culturally inferior (Carey, 1792). His fight with Hindu practices had evangelistic goals. His unwillingness to oppose the government's political and economic acts had mission and monetary aims. Carey failed to understand the colonial structure through which mission was nourished.

In contrast to Carey, Christian Schwartz worked 50 years before Carey reached India in the King of Tanjore's court as an administrator. He worked as a diplomat for King Tulajee. Like Carey he knew a considerable number of languages. He established some churches in the south east with his own money. He served as a mediator when Haider Ali sided with the French and considered war with the British. He was a friend of everyone. Haider Ali asked Schwartz, during the Carnatic war, to represent Britain, saying, 'Let them send me the Christian; he will not deceive me' (Firth, 1961). When dying, King Tulajee asked Schwartz to raise his own adopted son Saroboji. Saroboji wrote to the East India Company after Schwartz's death, saying, 'Oh, Gentlemen, that you were but able to send missionaries who would resemble the departed Schwartz!' (Mayhew, 1931).

Another significant European missionary was Alexander Duff. However, at this time among missionary societies the desire for Indian people to be converted was so important that there was no consideration about either people's rights or needs. Indian people's customs and religious beliefs were considered signs of their depravity. When the East India Company's Charter was renewed in 1833, missionaries were allowed to stay freely and free trade was also established. 'The missionaries asserted that since God had laid upon Britain the solemn duty of evangelizing India, the Government should not hesitate to throw its weight into the struggle. They demanded above all open Government patronage of Christian education and vigorous warfare upon the abuses associated with the Hindu religion' (Metcalf, 1964).

When Thomas Macaulay introduced English education to India in 1835 he had calculated that European science would remove local faiths in 40 years and would not only 'purge [India] of Hindu and Islamic religion, but also build up a new India with an essentially Christian constitution' (Mayhew, 1931). Alexander Duff felt the introduction of European science into education was value neutral; it should also include Christian instruction. When Lord Auckland supported other faiths' buildings with collection of a pilgrim tax in 1841, Duff wrote him a letter telling him to continue supporting Christianity alone. The letter refers to Indians as 'this benighted people' and to Islam as an 'idolatrous, pantheistic' religion. By 1854 there were 180 English schools and colleges, mostly run by missionaries with 30,000 students attending. But all these, except Benares, were within 300 miles of Calcutta. To an extent English education helped the local urban elites in Bengal (by this time an impoverished area) but the majority of underprivileged rural masses were untouched.

To reach their evangelistic goal, missionaries argued, people should introduce a European form of reformation in India. Duff reasoned, 'What the Christian Reformation did for Europe through the Greek tongue, the Roman Law and the Bible in the vernaculars, it will similarly do for India and further Asia through the English language and the British Administration' (Smith, n.d.). This reverses biblical and missiological order. Bible order is from inside to outside, but this is from outside to inside. Yet evangelicals preached the opposite, that only through being born again could a person be changed and through them could society be changed. Duff speaks of what he expected converts to Christianity to say, 'Woe be unto us if the British government were destroyed and the Hindu dynasties restored.... We pray for the permanence of the British government that, under the shadow of its protection, we may disseminate the healing knowledge of Christianity among our brethren....' Of such potential loyalty Duff writes, 'So clearly and strongly did this appear to many members of the present government in India, that instead of regarding us with jealousy and suspicion as enemies, they looked upon us as the truest friends of the British government, the staunchest supporters of the British power'.

Ignoring what imperialism had done in enriching Britain and impoverishing India, William Wilberforce saw India as sunk in the depths of moral wretchedness and degradation. He said that Britain's success was due to its religious and moral superiority and advocated receiving the light of the Gospel as the way forward for India (Dharampal, 1999).

In summary, nineteenth-century Christian mission, as well as colonial ideology, incorporated an isolation theology and politics of prejudice. Nineteenth-century mission was a structure formed in an imperial context. 'Colonial mission worked through domination to shape the style and content of missiography; there is no nineteenth-century mission policy, no evangelistic structure that has stood free of imperial, cultural and political formations that give colonial mission its peculiar individuality' (Dharmaraj, 1993).

Conclusions

This domination has created in the minds and hearts of African, Asian and Latin American people a love/hate relationship with white people. There is a love for white privilege, achievements, potential and materialist wealth. But there is also a hatred that white people through their greed and selfishness will do everything possible to deny access to those benefits to African, Asian and Latin American people, so they have little chance of gaining those benefits. The picture is of a bully who explains to you all the benefits of eating a beautiful apple and then puts it back in his pocket (Wright, 1964). Effectively, white people have turned the whole world against them. When they try to develop relationships with Majority World peoples now it's a bit like having the Midas touch. Majority World people are wary of developing relationships with white people because history tells us that Majority World people risk getting killed off (Haley, 1991). And when Black and Asian people try to get their money back somehow, perhaps by stealing, or some dubious business such as drug trafficking, white people say that this is against God's law, yet ignore that it is by breaking God's and man's laws in these very ways that white people got Black and Asian people's resources in the first place.

With respect to Protestant Christian mission in Africa and India, the following are some conclusions that can be drawn.

There are several things this book is not. It is not a history of missions. It does not cover creative initiatives, such as the rediscovery of New Testament missionary principles by A. N. Groves, or the self-supporting, self-governing and self-extending principles of Henry Venn and Rufus Anderson. Nor do I go into the many praiseworthy efforts of missionaries to serve God that were frustrated by white settlers or governments. Examples here include the model community of Livingstonia in Africa and the Aborigines Protection Societies. Missionaries did good and they should not be criticized because this doing good was overwhelmed by non-Christian opposition (e.g. 1. Peter 3. 17). Much has been written on these aspects of missionary work. What I am concerned about here is how people that missionaries went to and shared their lives with viewed what the missionaries did. Sadly, the views are that a lot that missionaries did was bad. Nevertheless, Christians were right to go and share their faith. Arguably the most positive models were those of the Moravians. Some of the most effective work that missionaries did was teaching literacy and working with local people to translate the Bible.

Christianity, sadly, was seen as the faith of a dominating people. For that very reason the faith of the invader was rejected (Howell, 2001). There was little effective restraint posed by Christians on white settlers. Thomas Fowell Buxton, MP for Weymouth and a director of the London Missionary Society, who in 1823 had succeeded Wilberforce in heading the campaign to rid British colonies of enslavement, established the Aborigines Select Committee Inquiry in 1835. Setting its tone, he said, 'What have we Christians done for [the indigenous peoples]? We have usurped their lands, kidnapped, enslaved and murdered themselves. The greatest of their crimes is that they sometimes trespass into the lands of their forefathers; and the very greatest of their misfortunes is that they have ever become acquainted with Christians. Shame on such Christianity!' (Buxton, 1848).

Further, it would have been helpful if Christians had avoided dualism. This resulted in a number of issues. Predominantly the Christianity missionaries brought was an otherworldly one (focusing on going to heaven when you die) and one that seemed to support the status quo of white domination, providing no challenge to what white colonizers were doing in the country and presenting little hope for change in this life for indigenous believers, unless it was through their gaining materially from the missionaries.

Again, white people not only took Christian faith they also took an intellectual tradition that was critical of Christian faith. This is secularism. Lamin Sanneh (1993) and Mark Noll (1994) point out that over the last three hundred years Christians have largely been ineffective at dealing with the claims of first, reason, then science then secularism in explaining how to understand God. Because of dualism, Christian missionaries displayed that secularism unintentionally in their lifestyles. Africans and Asians saw through this because their worldviews and cultures were holistic.

Then, Christians failed to act as Paul had done when encountering people from a different culture. Paul learnt from local people through a process of dialogue (May, 1990); he learnt and respected the worldview and thought forms of people; he found a way of enculturating and contextualizing his understanding of the gospel into these people's way of thinking and shared the gospel in this way; he fought those who tried as Judaizers to enforce the traditional mainstream's view that turned the gospel into legalism in obeying the sending culture's way of life; he also moved swiftly to ordain elders and deacons and move on so that churches could do the full work of contextualizing their faith on their own.

The evidence is that missionaries reacted at least in part to the local mayhem caused by white invaders but also to what they believed about 'the Other'. So they rejected the worldviews and cultures of local people, acting as if they had little if anything to learn from them; sought to impose white, superior views of the gospel and life as a civilizing principle in place of existing worldviews and cultures; and acted as if communication was one way rather than a dialogue. I am aware that contextualization did become more important to white people from around the 1970s.

Further, local people saw little evidence of challenge on the part of missionaries' supporters in the white people's home country towards the government about the effects of colonialism abroad. These effects included violence, injustice, capitalism, racism, sexism and classism. The exception is the movement to abolish enslavement, although this seemed to develop mass support only after white people had been involved for at least two hundred years. The general lack of challenge to governments may be due to various of the reasons above but it also throws doubt on how churches view their involvement in intercultural ministry.

Again, there is evidence that missionary societies not only modeled themselves on the joint-stock company, but that they also took the ethos of both transnational companies and white people's neo-liberalism into their ministries and into the lives of Christians and churches abroad.

Also, as Guha (1992) indicates, Christians who are subordinate to white dominators are involved in continual resistance in order to achieve liberation from white domination. This means that not only do they construct their identity and self actualisation in the light of white domination but also they construct their theology as a reaction to white domination and taking into account their struggle for liberation.

Let's hear the last word from a Latin American. Orlando Costas (1983), a Puerto Rican, concludes of white missionaries' work that God's Word was shared in a language foreign to the hearers' cultures and socio-economic experience; Jesus was preached not only out of touch with local societies but also out of touch with the New Testament; that liturgies, architecture, art forms and music were white. He is not surprised that not more than 3% of Asian people came to follow Jesus and that Africa and Latin America saw the growth of independent churches protesting at the foreignness of how the gospel was proclaimed.

Chapter 4
A common Black experience: post-traumatic slave syndrome

'So the beginning of this was a woman and she had come back from burying the dead. Not the dead of sick and ailing and friends at the pillow and the feet. She had come back from the sodden and the bloated; the sudden dead, their eyes flung wide open in judgment' (Hurston, 1937).

'Racism as white supremacy has been the reality that Black people all over this planet have faced for the last 500 years. There's never been a moment, there's never been a minute, there's never been a day, there's never been a week where we haven't been confronted with racism as a system. Never a half a minute' (Cress Welsing, 2010).

'Oppression refers to the constraints and the deep injustice that are part of unquestioned norms, habits, symbols and assumptions present in the ordinary behaviours of people, in media and cultural stereotypes, and in the structural features of organizations, institutional living, bureaucratic hierarchies and market mechanisms. There are different causes for, as well as kinds of, oppression, all of them equally unjust: exploitation, marginalization, powerlessness, cultural imperialism, and systemic violence' (Isasi-Diaz, 2000).

Introduction

Here I show that, while many in the Majority World have suffered trauma through colonialism and globalization, the trauma and psychological problems suffered by Black people during enslavement and subsequently in the Western Hemisphere and afterwards in UK have been particularly harrowing. I use African-Caribbean contributions from Roy Heath and Barbara Fletchman Smith, with a UK case study.

Chapter 2 showed that there is a need for white people to learn from the new centre of the church, Black, Asian and Latin American people, the people of the Majority world. Where we start is the place where we as peoples have got to in our engagement with each other. I covered this in chapters 1-3 of *CG*. So as not to repeat myself, yet so as to help people get a sense of where we have got to, I will introduce here one result of the first encounter between white people and African people – post-traumatic slave syndrome.

As a people we sometimes don't find it easy to recognize that what some people might have gone through might have caused them to experience trauma. There is, however, an attempt to recognize that people need to learn not to repeat violent acts in the British government's recognition of an annual day to commemorate the

Jewish Holocaust. This reminds us of the German military's acts to kill 11 million people, including six million Jews, and also Poles, other ethnic groups, homosexuals and disabled people during the Second World War.

The British army is still struggling to come to grips with the nature of Gulf War Syndrome. This is characterized by symptoms of fatigue, muscle pain, cognitive problems, rashes and diarrhoea. 35% of US war veterans of the first Gulf War are estimated to be suffering from this syndrome. Worryingly, many US veterans of subsequent wars in Iraq and Afghanistan are also believed to be suffering from this syndrome. There are specific physical causes, for example exposure to chemical weapons, which distinguish syndrome sufferers from those who do not suffer. A major reason for defence ministries' dragging their feet in recognizing the existence of people suffering from Gulf War Syndrome is the expectation that there may need to be significant financial compensation of sufferers as a result of recognizing the syndrome.

Following acceptance of the existence of Gulf War Syndrome many people have come to take seriously a wider range of experiences as contributing towards the experience of Post Traumatic Stress Disorder (PTSD). People open to the experience of PTSD are those who might have experienced trauma as a result of a wide variety of experiences, including military combat, surviving a concentration camp, experiencing a violent crime or natural disaster. Characteristic symptoms of PTSD are re-experiences of trauma through flashbacks, leading to significant impairment in a person's social relationships.

But many will say, 'Slavery finished 180 years ago in the Caribbean. How can anyone be suffering from trauma as a result of slavery today?' There are a number of reasons why people can still be suffering trauma.

Psychological problems can be passed down from one generation to the next and beyond. A family I know of have similar psychological problems on both sides of the family going back at least 130 years and those psychological problems have now been passed on to their children, therefore continuing through four generations.

Further, trauma is perpetuated as people change their lifestyles to adopt survival strategies to respond to the trauma experienced. DeGruy Leary (2005) points, for example, to Black children to this day in US being forced by their mother to stay close to her at the bank while white children are allowed to do anything they please. The message this sends is that this world belongs to white boys and girls, who may do as they please in the world, but not to Black boys and girls. If Black boys and girls play around at the bank, there might well be a reaction from white people.

Again, when the experience of terror is repeated over the intervening years subsequently, in the form of structured and systemic racism and oppression, trauma is reinforced.

For example, in the U.S., following emancipation from enslavement in 1863 and after the respite of reconstruction, there followed the imposition of Jim Crow segregation laws in the South and lynchings throughout the country. Following Civil Rights laws in the 1960s and another brief respite, mass unemployment of Blacks resulted from moving jobs to the Majority World from 1975 onwards. Poor areas of the U.S. were neglected economically, yet came under close police surveillance. In the name of waging a 'War on Drugs' many young Black men have been put in prison. Michelle Alexander (2012) speaks of these conditions as *The New Jim Crow*.

In the Caribbean, where many islands were to remain colonies until the middle of the twentieth century, European nations decided that there was to be a 'new deal for the planters'. Slave owners were compensated for losing their slaves: emancipated slaves received no compensation for slavery. The Act of Emancipation of 1834 contained the provision for the employment of indentured labour: large numbers of people were brought from India and China to the Caribbean. These people were paid low wages but their presence and the merging of many plantations resulted in high unemployment for emancipated Africans. This caused conditions of great hardship for African-Caribbeans for a hundred years after emancipation.

Further, migration, for example from the Caribbean to the U.K, causes a disruption to the process of healing from trauma. It involves separation from loved ones who might never be seen again. It also breaks traditional ties of loyalty to one's own culture. When it results in losing the presence of a father figure, it may result in a child finding it difficult to separate from their mother (Fletchman Smith, 2003).

Many will say, 'You can't say I'm responsible for slavery! I've never done anything like that!' Sadly, however, many people's attitudes and behaviour towards people they see as different from, perhaps inferior to, themselves have not changed much more than becoming less overt, more covert over the intervening years. Today, it's discrimination that keeps many people around the world poor, while some may benefit from this and become richer.

Although I have focused on trauma caused by white people to Black people in the Western Hemisphere, some of whom have since migrated to Europe, this is only a part of the trauma caused by colonialism and globalization. A friend of mine refers to this wider trauma as 'Postcolonial trauma syndrome'. Watkins and Shulman (2010) bring case studies from around the world to show the damage and wounds caused by colonial and globalization to Majority World people and routes that can lead people to psychic and social emancipation (Martin-Baro, 1994).

Some Christians might say, 'Christians weren't responsible for what happened to African people in the Western Hemisphere'. It would be right to say that there might have been some ways in which some Christians behaved better towards Majority

World people than non-Christians did. But we need to look, for example, in US at behaviour during enslavement, during Reconstruction, during the Jim Crow segregation period, during the lynching period, and in discriminating against Black, Native American, Asian and Latino peoples economically. We need to see in the Caribbean the marginalization of Black people between emancipation and independence and the favouring of light-skinned people over dark-skinned people since then. And we need to see the way in which the church in Latin American countries lined up alongside the landowners and the state in opposing human rights for ordinary people, although there appears to have been a long-standing resistance by clergy and church attendees in poor areas (Gonzalez, 1990). There is not much evidence from Black, Native American and Latino people that white Christians come out of these situations with much more credit than white non-Christians.

While some have struggled to understand the reasons for continuing psychological problems among oppressed people, many people have not found it hard to understand the continuing life-changing financial benefit to the families of slave owners. For example, General Sir James Duff, David Cameron's first cousin six times removed, received 4101 pounds, or over 3 million pounds in today's money, for 202 slaves that he received compensation for forfeiting at emancipation, from Grange Sugar Estate, Jamaica (Draper et al., 2014).

African enslavement in the Western Hemisphere
Portuguese travels along the west coast of Africa in the 15th century resulted from the need to find a sea route through which to trade with India following Muslims blocking the overland route. The Portuguese were driven by the principles of capitalism, a desire to buy cheap and sell dear (Sivanandan, 1982).

Columbus' subsequent discovery of the Western Hemisphere in 1492 identified bases from which large scale production could be developed to sell to an export market (Williams, 1994). With such a large area of land, capitalists found that voluntary workers preferred to buy their own land and develop their own smallholding rather than work hard for the capitalist.

Initially, indigenous peoples were forced to work in growing businesses, but the change of lifestyle, together with succumbing to European diseases and in some cases killings meant that indigenous peoples could not be relied on to provide cheap labour for large-scale production. Many white people came as indentured servants to the Western Hemisphere. They preferred long-term to own and develop their own smallholdings and this resulted in their feeling forced to leave some areas by the move to develop large plantations there.

Africans were therefore transported from, predominantly West, Africa to the Western Hemisphere because they were the cheapest labour that could be got to enable large-scale production. The process of enforced enslavement and transportation across Africa, transportation across the middle passage of the Atlantic and chattel slavery in the Western Hemisphere for over 400 years was horrific, even for those days. The Trans-Atlantic Slave Trade Database (http://www.slavevoyages.org/tast/index.faces) estimated that 10.7 million Africans arrived in the Western Hemisphere from Africa.

Around 2 million people are estimated to have died during the middle passage. It is difficult to speculate how many might have died before being shipped from Africa. Conservative estimates are 7 million. Some figures for the total of African people who died in Africa are much higher. To get many more slaves than by raiding villages themselves, European slave traders in Africa sold weapons to local rulers and encouraged them to fight their neighbour. William Pitt condemned this in Parliament in 1792 (Williams, 1940). In these wars to gain slaves, as many Africans were killed as were captured alive (Hart, 1998).

While 10.7 million people in the Western Hemisphere might not sound many, modern repercussions could be significant. For example, the database estimates that only 450,000 of these came to the area today known as U.S. However, today's African-American population has grown to 42 million (Gates, 2014).

The common practice in the Caribbean was to work slaves as hard as possible, so maximizing production in the short term, and to rely on replacing these with new slaves from Africa (Parliamentary Papers, 1790-1). John Newton, a slave trader who subsequently became an Anglican minister, quoted an Antiguan slave planter in 1751 who said it was common on the island for slaves not to stay alive there more than nine years (Newton, 1788).

Common experiences during enslavement

Karenga (1993) makes the case that when we look at all the holocausts of history, none surpasses that of white people's chattel enslavement of African people over more than 400 years, in terms of genocide, the destruction of cultures and heritage and the inflicting of ongoing social death on African people.

Enslavement was organized for the domination, ownership and exploitation of one person by another. Transported Africans suffered the loss of their connection to Africa, their family relationships, their name and language. Relationships were distorted between white people and Africans, particularly between white men and African women. Enslavement brought a divide between African men and women: the white slave owner delegated power to the African woman to stop the African man being the controller of the family's development. Finally, white women came to hate the African woman, who was seen as a threat to the white woman's happiness with her husband (Fletchman Smith, 2011).

As the individual comes to accept enslavement, they realize they are regulated by something external with sadistic power. This is the opposite of feeling you are free to be self-regulating. If you believe you are powerless to change the sadistic power of an external world, your life becomes one of mental slavery (Douglass, 1955). This is a mental condition that is still very common. While there were slave rebellions, most people were worn down by the violence used to keep enslavement going.

For women, slavery meant that work had a higher priority than motherhood, up until the1807 Abolition of the Slave Trade. This was enslavement's attempt to overthrow the order of family life practiced by the rest of the world. Male and female bodies were not their own and were interfered with. For example, in his journals from 1748-1786, Thomas Thistlewood, a slave planter in Jamaica, records 3852 sexual acts he did with 138 different women, almost all being enslaved Africans. It is difficult to understand these acts as anything other than rape (Burnard, 2004).

African women had equality of treatment with men in their work load and also in their inhumane treatment. The lack of protection that they got from African men from the sexual actions of white men contributed towards their lasting attitude of independence of and scornfulness towards men generally.

Slave-owning staff, specifically white men, inserted themselves into African male and female couples. This 'third person', who possessed power, disturbed conditions of loyalty and trust in relationships, interfering with people's desires to be free, to marry and form families.

The biggest disaster for Africans was the diminution of power of the African man in the family. The African woman bore a child for the African man or the white man and got back to work. The African man became implicated in the abuse of the African woman, because he was unable to defend and protect her against rape. All the children were the property of the slave owner, who would sell them at any time. These arrangements induced terror, a feeling of helplessness and ongoing trouble for African men trying to claim their place in a family with their wife and children. As a result, African men tended to become more withdrawn and depressed, while African women became more disturbed and angry (Bush, 1990). Both often manifested as psychological problems.

For African women, mothering interfered with work in the fields, so, sadly, mothering lost out. The consequences of this were severe for the mental health of women and children. Under pressure from the slave owner to increase the number of their children, African women took power over their bodies to resist oppressors. They used sexual abstinence as well as different contraceptive methods to avoid having children (Bush, 1990). As a result, in the Caribbean the number of Africans did not increase, although it did increase in the southern US, where the number of Africans shipped directly from Africa was far less than in the Caribbean. While male action to slow the birth rate has not been investigated, it is possible that homosexual activity may be part of the explanation.

African women who had relationships with white men were able to raise their social standing by so doing, starting with a move from working in the fields to working in the plantation house. The people who lost out were white women, who were under increasing competition from African women, and African men, who wanted women. Enslavement was responsible for the change in power relations between African men and women. African men lost rights over their children through no fault of their own. Through this they also lost responsibility for them as well. These changes in relationships contributed towards a general lack of support towards women and children.

Continuing results of enslavement

Sigmund Freud (1900) identified that in the life of every child there comes a time when they encounter the Oedipus complex and need to find a way to resolve it. According to the story *Oedipus Rex* by Sophocles, Oedipus kills his father and marries his mother. For Freud, the Oedipus complex is a time for the child to deal with their passions towards their parents or guardians of incest and murder.

In enslavement, white people treated black people as sub-human. This enabled white people not to feel guilty about acting out incest and murder with black people. The slave owner acted as the 'father' with the slaves being his 'children'. The result of enslavement for black children was that very often they did not know who their parents, grandparents and other relatives were. Separation of children from parents and of husbands from wives led on to men seeing sex as a means of satisfying their masculinity without any responsibility for looking after their children. The separation of procreation from paternity resulted in Black people acting as a babyfather or babymother rather than as a married couple.

Families were finding some way of coping with these pressures within extended families when large-scale migration from the Caribbean to US and UK began from the middle of the twentieth century. Very often grandparents were left behind in the Caribbean. Mothers prioritized work over care as they had done during enslavement. In the UK the dominant type of Caribbean family is single-parent families, with the mother the chief breadwinner. Again children often do not know who their father is, or their siblings or their ancestors.

Memory of trauma creates severe feelings of fear, through memories of castration anxiety, whether actual or symbolic. This fear, generated through the mother-infant relationship, makes it difficult for the child to resolve the Oedipus complex. The child's future stability will depend on their mastery of loving over hating their mother. Normal Oedipal feelings of rivalry that a boy has for his father may become so distorted by a mother's contemptuousness towards his father that male identification and solidarity is disrupted. This and any actual absence of a loving father weakens a son's masculinity and feeling of internal male protection. This produces anxiety in the presence of women and hatred of them. So women are hated because they are feared. A girl in the absence of a loving father often has a problem with boundaries. A serious delay of sexual object choice may result in a position of bisexuality becoming fixed.

Super-ego development is frustrated when the Oedipus complex is not resolved. The super-ego is the means by which conscience develops. The super-ego contains prohibitions and a sense of morality that comes from a child's parents. This failure to internalize prohibitions and a lack of conscience has led a growing number of young men and women into criminal activity. Research shows that third- and fourth-generation African Caribbean youth in UK have a higher incidence of psychotic illness than other groups (King et al., 1994). There is a high incidence of young men from this background in secure units and prisons.

An inability of the child to separate from their mother at the Oedipal moment occurs when the child is separated from their mother at a young age, is brought up by a different family or is sent away from their home country by their parents (Robertson and Robertson, 1989; Mahler et al., 1975). The child then tries to find the love of a mother and father but is frustrated. Unless this child is able to come to terms with what has happened and move on through psychotherapy this can lead to ongoing problems throughout their life.

Rosine Perelberg (1999) gives frameworks for understanding violence. When thinking about violence on the part of some young people we need to remember that serious anger at injustice and racism has not gone away. Some will fight to hang on to livelihoods of buying and selling drugs. These young people will probably have good impulse control. Those with little impulse control will be those who have struggles with defining and defending their masculinity. There is a long history of this in the Caribbean, explained well by Earl Lovelace (1979). In the UK, Winnicott (1984) makes the connection between deprivation, a tendency to be anti-social and absence of guilt. Often a young person will suffer from a lack of good care, paternal absence and the bereavement of close friends. This might result in their becoming devoted to committing crime just to stay alive.

Carolyn West (2008) analyses three common stereotypes that white people have of Black women. The first is that of a subordinate, nurturing, self-sacrificing Mammy figure. Enslaved women were often overworked, beaten and raped. However, in response they helped other slaves escape or ran away themselves, many fought back when punished while some poisoned slave owners. This was an uncomfortable reality, so authors and historians rewrote history so as to create the image of the happy, loyal Mammy. If we could believe the Mammy in *Gone with the wind* was content in her life, this might help us believe that enslavement was humane.

The second stereotype is that of a sexually promiscuous Jezebel. When African women arrived in the US they were put on the auction block, stripped naked and their reproductive capacity was examined. After they were sold, they were bribed, forced, seduced, commanded and finally violently forced into sexual relations with not only slave owners but their sons, relatives and overseers. After enslavement finished, vigilante groups like the Ku Klux Klan during the lynching years in all states raped Black women.

The third stereotype is that of the Sapphire. Black women were pictured as strong workhorses who worked alongside Black men in the fields or as aggressive women, driving both their partner and their children away with their overbearing nature. In reality, it was slave-owners who sold their children and husbands away, causing women tremendous pain and anger. Their partner's absence caused the woman to take on the traditional role of the man, such as providing financially. However, social scientists have claimed it is Black women's domination as matriarchs in families, rather than discrimination in social policies and economic inequality, which were responsible for unemployment and emasculation of Black men, which resulted in single parenthood, poverty and producing underachieving and criminally inclined Black children (Collins, 2000). People need to do research into Black women's daily experiences of anger. These are often fuelled by racism, lack of power, respect and control (Fields et al., 1998, Harris-Perry, 2011).

Fletchman Smith (2003) analyses the character of Galton Flood in Roy Heath's *The murderer* (1984), set in Guyana, to identify both how psychotic breakdown develops and the developmental factors facilitating paranoia.

Galton's problems largely stem from his upbringing by his parents. Galton's mother wears down his father and controls Galton's movements so he is used to staying at home. The fear that Galton has is what was instilled into men during enslavement. It has been internalized and contributes to castration anxiety. Galton's mother brings into the marriage scorn and hatred of men who failed to protect women during enslavement. She also bullies Galton's father and Galton, as the slave owner's bullying has also been internalized. Slavery reduced both men and women, but it reduced men more than it did women. Women emerged from enslavement knowing their potential power, e.g. in seducing the slave owner, raising their living standards, raising children, and enriching both plantation and owner. From age three, Galton is told of his father's sin and shame and his own fear, while his mother asks him to make his father a better man for her benefit.

Galton's mother's action is one of trying to pull Galton into a partnership with her against his father, while his father avoids conflict with her, thus pushing Galton away from him. These actions cause increased hostility by Galton against both his parents. Galton and his mother are thus unable to lead separate lives because of his father's failure to insert himself between them. Galton is unable to build a true self but has to set up a false self to fit his mother's wishes, but which leaves him open to psychosis. The situation is not helped by the absence of grandparents. Galton's father and mother then both die within a year of each other when Galton is in his late adolescence. Later in life, Galton marries Gemma but his inability to develop relationships with women eventually leads him to kill her.

Cultures that have experienced enslavement keep a memory that all men are useless. Case studies show that girls suffer where no father is present in their lives.

Case study

Fletchman Smith (2003) uses a number of very helpful case studies from her work in UK which make concrete some of the issues we have mentioned.

For example, Miss C. was the eldest child born in the UK to parents who had migrated to UK from the Caribbean. Their other children had been left behind with relatives in the Caribbean. The family moved in with an uncle in a house peopled with their relatives. Miss C. was born there and the family lived in one room. The family missed the children and grandmothers left behind. Miss C's mother had neither her children nor her mother by her side.

With both parents out at work, when Miss C. was home someone in the house would look after her. Miss C's father was diagnosed as schizophrenic and spent increasingly long stays in hospital. Miss C's mother may have colluded in his isolation. In this connection, Fletchman Smith quotes McDougall (1989) in saying that the father's presence is important in enabling the infant to cope with the fact of difference and the task of separating his or her own mind, sex and body from the mind, sex and body of the mother.

Miss C's father grew up with his mother after his father died in an accident when he was three. Miss C's widowed grandmother was a woman in touch with the supernatural (Obeah) and tied her son to herself with magical powers. She disapproved of his marriage to Miss C's mother.

Before the marriage, Miss C's father had tried to escape his mother by travelling to work in other parts of the Caribbean and the US. He used to return to her, putting money into a bank account that she kept for him. His mother died just after he had first been in a psychiatric hospital in UK. He was depressed to find she had spent all the money in his account. Fletchman Smith feels that the hatred Miss C's father had towards his mother both made it difficult for him to have protective feelings towards Miss C. and also literally sent her father mad.

Miss C's mother had parents who never married: her father was already promised to a different woman when he met Miss C's mother, so he did not stay with her. Miss C's mother therefore grew up without a father, being brought up by her mother and grandmother, so probably without any experience of closeness to a male family member. So both of Miss C's parents grew up without their fathers being around, and with no experience of a heterosexual couple.

While Miss C. was living in the house owned by the uncle she was sexually abused at least three times. Once she was left alone with her uncle who had full intercourse with her. He threatened her with further assaults if she told her mother. Once Miss C. was left with a female family friend locally, who left her with a male family member, who was visiting, who assaulted her. She was subsequently assaulted by the same man and a visiting friend of the family.

Miss C's family was re-housed by the Council, first in a flat, then in a house. While in the lift going up to her parents' flat she witnessed the assault of a female cousin the same age as her by a man who had previously abused Miss C.

Miss C. was unable to tell her father or mother about the abuse. She once told her mother she was 'hurting in the middle'. Her mother took her to the doctor who recommended she changed what she drank. Neither doctor nor mother examined her. Miss C. completed a university degree. Fearing unemployment less than living alone and dying of emotional starvation she returned to live at home and got a job.

Miss C. began to experience physical problems. She had blocked sinuses and a constantly runny nose, while mucus came through her eyes when she blew her nose. An ENT specialist recommended surgery, in which the lining of her nostrils was removed. However the blocked sinuses and runny nose continued.

After this failed surgery, she first saw 'the faces dream'. The dream was of three clouds floating across her room, each with a face in the middle. The first time she saw it she screamed and her mother came running. Her family reacted by deciding to respond to the spirits they believed were bothering Miss C., rather than attending to Miss C. It was suggested that because her bed was facing the door this was encouraging the spirits to interfere with her. Someone interfering was thus projected onto 'bad spirits'. The family said she should hide from the spirits by placing her bed so that its head blocked the room's entrance, so that she was facing the wall. By co-operating with the family, Fletchman Smith felt Miss C. was trying to stop the trauma forcing itself into her consciousness and destroying her mind.

After three years Miss C. got a painful shoulder from how she was sleeping. Since she had been anally abused, when she turned over to lie on her other side she felt she left herself open to attack. It was partly to gain relief from this that Miss C. came to Fletchman Smith for help.

Two years before the initial consultation, Miss C's parents had separated, although the family did not openly acknowledge this. Miss C's father had gone into community care permanently. Miss C and her mother then bought the council house. Miss C's anger with her mother began to grow, owing to her mother's lack of appreciation of Miss C's efforts to please and also because her mother imposed on her financially and emotionally. Both Miss C and her mother had become very anxious about separation. Since Miss C had missed out on age-appropriate attention from her parents she had now effectively formed a couple with her mother. She was able to make sadistic attacks on her mother, although these might in turn also drive her mad.

Miss C. was forming a sadomasochistic couple with her mother. This reaches back to the time when African-Caribbeans were angry with Africans for failing to protect them from abuse and for co-operating with white people in their enslavement.

Miss C. eventually responded well to psychoanalytic psychotherapy, primarily because of the educated upbringing she had had. Fletchman Smith comments that childhood sexual abuse, of girls and boys, is often spoken of by African-Caribbean and African-American writers. This is not surprising since enslavement was created so as to abuse human beings.

As a member of a Black Majority Church, I, weekly, see the struggles of people trying to forgive whoever has abused them in any way, verbal, physical, etc. If that other person dies without your trying to restore the relationship, it has been known to break people. It's humbling when people of my own background are the abusers.

Chapter 5
On becoming the global rich

'Racism... remains a powerful system that we're immediately born into. It's like being born into air: you take it in as soon as you breathe. It's not a cold that you can get over. There is no anti-racist certification class. It's a set of socioeconomic traps and cultural values that are fired up every time we interact with the world. It is a thing you have to keep scooping out of the boat of your life to keep from drowning in it. I know it's hard work, but it's the price you pay for owning everything' (Woods, 2014).

'What you hear in my voice is fury, not suffering. Anger, not moral authority' (Lorde, 1984).

'I watched that dream turn into a nightmare as I moved through the ghettos of the nation and saw my black brothers and sisters perishing on a lonely island of poverty in the midst of a vast ocean of material prosperity, and saw the nation really doing nothing to grapple with the Negroes' problem of poverty' (King, 1967).

(In the US) 'analyzing data from the Study of Women's Health from Across the Nation (SWAN), we estimate that at ages 49-55, Black women are 7.5 years biologically older than white women. Indicators of perceived stress and poverty account for 27% of this difference.... Further investigation ... is merited' (National Centre for Biotechnology Information, 2010).

Introduction

I outline here some ways that the West has made itself rich at the expense of the Majority World and make comparisons with the Jewish nation of Jesus' day. I do some Bible study on poverty and wealth. I consider how one missionary kid (MK) responded to poverty. I consider how white people can act to change the system and approach racial reconciliation.

One of my biggest challenges is meeting Christian leaders who challenge me deeply with their spirituality and have in their home a son who has made a profession of faith and perhaps has been baptized. I don't know whether he did well at school or not, but today he is out of work or works intermittently and suffers from depression. He may well have seen a good friend shot or knifed to death. And he often appears to have given up on church. In predominantly African-Caribbean churches, for example, up to 80%-90% of the congregation may be female. I am sure that there are many reasons as to why men no longer worship God in church.

Asians also are leaving churches because of the pain they receive from their experience of church. Sometimes church leaders can be very restrictive on young people from their community and young people decide to leave. But I believe everyone has dreams of achieving their potential. And I am convinced that African and Asian young men give up on church often because in the face of racism they meet in society related to, for example, the practicalities of getting and keeping a job that matches their skills they feel that the church fails to work with them sufficiently in overcoming and exposing that racism and helping them get a job, because of the otherworldly preoccupations of the church. The best place to recruit to the Nation of Islam in U.S. was always outside Black Majority Churches (Malcolm X, 2001). What challenges me most as I stand in any church service is how I can help to change the minds and hearts of potential employers and workmates and of the institutions of society towards young men like this one who aren't in church.

I explained in *CG* chapters 1 to 3 how Britain and the West grew in wealth as they went through their industrial revolutions. Many of these countries had gained an empire by force, establishing colonies in Africa, Asia and Latin America. They increased their wealth principally by taking the labour, land and resources of people of Majority World background for less than what they were worth. The ratio of income per person in developed countries vs. income per person in developing countries grew from 3:1 in 1820 to 72:1 in 1992 (United Nations Development Programme, 1999). That is, on average, people in developed countries earn and live on over 70 times as much money every day as people in developing countries. Today the richest 20% of the world's population has 75% of the world's wealth, while the poorest 80% of the world live on 25% of its wealth (United Nations, 2007).

It is now forecast that in 2016 the top 1% of the world's population will have more wealth than the other 99% of the world's population (Oxfam, 2015). However, the 70 million people in this top 1% own assets worth only 530,000 pounds, or the cost of an average London house. People like us could be in this top 1% (Reuben, 2015).

When Western Christians think about rich people, they usually think of rich celebrities as being 'the rich', rather than themselves, seeing themselves as 'just getting by'. While it is true that many celebrities will certainly be richer than them, Western Christians must face up to the fact that in relation to the majority of people in the world, Western Christians are also part of the global rich.

Comparing this world situation with the Palestine of Jesus' lifetime, the richest 5% of that country's people controlled 65% of its wealth, the remaining 95% of people shared 35% of its wealth (Hanson and Oakman, 1998). The ruling elite were 3% of the population, merchants and artisans 12%, 75% peasants and 10% unclean (Kraybill, 2003). Taxes, cost of seed and rent cost peasants 90% of their income, so they had to live off the remaining 10% (Oakman, 1986). So there are some similarities between the polarisation of income in the world today and that in the Palestine of Jesus' day.

The two main reasons for this poverty in New Testament times were Roman power and Jewish leaders' power, expressed by making themselves rich through taking the money of most Jewish people. This ties in with findings from other times in history, including the present, that there is an international element of the oppression and a national element of the oppression.

Internationally, Rome took 25% of peasants' income as a land tax. In addition, Roman soldiers, who were all Roman citizens, were allowed to retire after 25 years' service in the country where they served and take a large area of land to live on.

Nationally, Jews had got used to paying high taxes to Herod the Great for his public works, like rebuilding the Temple. People estimate that Herod the Great had owned 65% of the country. The Herodians' power, however, was waning by the time of Jesus' ministry. The scribes and Pharisees were growing in power, that power being based around the synagogue system across the country, where they were the rabbis and judged legal disputes. The temple was the main source of income generation and distribution in the country, so the most powerful group in the country was the Jewish clerical aristocracy, comprising the priests, elders and Sadducees, who between them controlled the Sanhedrin. Over time most peasants were taxed out of their homes and had to pay 50% of their income to their absent landowner on an ongoing basis. 25% of their income went to the Romans, while 10% went to the Jewish clerical aristocracy for upkeep of the Temple. Taking off seed and other costs peasants therefore had to live on 10% of their income. Publicans were responsible for collecting all the taxes and did so while levying their own fees for the collection.

Jesus' message of a full jubilee for the poor was therefore a challenge to the livelihood of all these powerful people (Gonzalez, 2002; Kraybill, 2003).

Implications for white Christians of becoming the global rich
Jonathan Bonk (1996) has produced a useful outline of Bible teaching on poverty and wealth. In the OT there is some teaching that the rich find in their favour. It is alright to have private property; the righteous will prosper; sometimes people are to blame if they become poor; wealth has advantages to poverty. However, most of this (Proverbs, Ecclesiastes) is written by Solomon, a tremendously wealthy king who oppressed his people against God's guidelines for kings (Deut. 17: 14-20), resulting in God taking 10 tribes away from his son (2 Chron. 10: 1-19). Most Old Testament teaching is more disturbing for rich people. For God's people, it is not to be their purpose to go from birth to death in the most comfortable way (Job 1: 21); use of personal wealth is subordinated to caring for poorer people, for example, through returning land at the jubilee, so that everybody has equal shares of land (Lev. 25: 8-43); canceling debts in the seventh year (Lev. 25: 1-7; Deut. 15: 1-11);

75

giving tithes (Deut. 14: 22-29; 26: 1-15); charging no interest on a loan (Lev. 25: 35-38); gleaning (Deut. 24: 19-20) and treatment of employees (Deut. 24: 14-15).

Wealth is dangerous spiritually: it tempts people to ignore God (Deut. 8: 1-20); gives false security (Prov. 10: 15); is the enemy of humility (Jer. 9: 23-24); the rich are susceptible to sins like greed (Eccles. 5: 8-15); abuse of power (1 Kings 21: 1-16); contempt for the poor (Jer. 22: 13-17). Discontent with what you have is the root of overindulgence (Ps. 73: 25-26). Desire for wealth corrupts people who speak for God (Num. 22). In the Old Testament, wealth is normally achieved through unrighteousness (Job 21: 7-16); the rich are often responsible for the situation of the poor (Prov. 13: 23); preoccupation with material advancement brings disaster (2. Kings 5: 15-27); oppression of the poor leads to judgment (Mic. 2: 1-3); orthodoxy without justice is a sham (Is. 1: 10-23).

Oppression is a common, if neglected, theme in the Bible. Crucially, God identifies with oppressed people and might crush oppressors (Ps. 10: 17-18; 72: 4; Is. 14. 1-6); the Messiah comes as an oppressed person (Is. 53: 1-12); oppressors cannot claim to be children of God (Ps. 37: 21-28); righteousness shows itself through concern for the poor (Amos 5: 4-24); God meets poor people's needs through the action of God's obedient people (Neh. 5: 1-13); giving to God involves giving things people value (Mal. 1: 6-14); true repentance involves economic justice (Is. 58: 1-11).

Some New Testament teaching which rich people find reassures them includes that having private property is alright (Luke 4: 38); some followers of Jesus were rich (Matt. 27: 57-60); and Jesus commends businessmen for their investments (Luke 19: 11-27). Most New Testament economic teaching, however, is distressing to the rich.

Accumulation of wealth is not a worthwhile life goal. White people today share good news that they consider important yet are unwilling to share the possessions they consider unimportant (Luke 12: 34). Possessions are only good when they promote Christ's cause (Luke 14: 12-14). Jesus said it is almost impossible for rich people to get to heaven (Mark 10: 17-31). Greed and swindling are seen similarly to idolatry: those that are greedy and swindlers will not go to heaven (1 Cor. 6: 9-10).

Wealth is dangerous (Matt. 10: 5-10; 18: 1-9). Jesus identified himself with poor people in his life and ministry (Luke 1: 46-56; 4: 16-19; 6: 20-26; Phil. 2: 1-11). Repentance for the rich is possible, although rare (Luke 19: 1-9). White Christians who see themselves as leaders of the worldwide church, risk being in a situation similar to the Pharisees (Matt. 23: 23-26).

Case study: the story of the Rich Man and Lazarus (Luke 16. 19-31)
Olubiyi Adeniyi Adewale (2006) comments usefully on this story. Jesus has been explaining to the Pharisees why he has been keeping company with sinners (15: 1-2). Jesus commends the shrewd use of money by non-Christians (16: 8), the

Pharisees sneer at him (16: 14) and Jesus warns the Pharisees and also his disciples about having the Pharisees' attitudes in the story of the Rich Man and Lazarus. Since the first part of the story seems taken from a Jewish folk-tale some commentators say we should focus on the message from the second half of the story (16: 27-31). However, Adewale argues for the parable's unity.

With respect to the rich man, for someone to be clothed in Egyptian cotton undergarments ('fine linen') and a robe coloured with Phoenician purple dye, daily (the force of the imperfect tense in *enediduske*) shows that he was very rich. His food was a daily banquet. Since his house had a gate it was probably either a compound or estate to match his riches.

With respect to Lazarus, the word used for poor indicates that he was a beggar with no support socially. The word translated 'who lay' is in the pluperfect tense and the passive voice and can be translated 'was thrown down'. It is often used to describe someone bedridden or crippled, as in Matt. 8: 6, 14; 9: 2 or Rev. 2: 22. So each day, Lazarus' friends laid him at the rich man's gate, hoping for some help. In African and other societies the rich man would be expected to help the poor in his community. Lazarus was 'full of sores'. The phrase 'desiring to be filled' is similar to those in Luke 15:16; 17:22 and 22:15. According to Jeremias (1954), the crumbs are those pieces of bread that the guests used to wipe their hands with before throwing them under the table for the dogs to eat (see Matt. 15: 27). The rich man saw the dogs as being more important than Lazarus: in African societies this would be seen as a great sin necessitating community reprisals against the rich man. Ironically Europeans subsidise their cows with more money each day than half the world has to live on. Almost half of the world's people live on less than $2.50 a day (World Bank, 2008), while Europeans daily subsidise their cows at a higher level, $2.62 a day (Elliott, 2005). Africans are also aware that dogs can help heal sores by licking them. This would indicate that in Lazarus' thinking the rich man is lower than the dogs, because the dogs helped him.

Abraham is used as a contrast to the rich man in the story, being a rich man who demonstrated by his attitude to material possessions that he had a right relationship with God. The implication in verse 30 that the problem was the rich man's brothers' lack of repentance shows that lack of repentance was the main problem with the rich man in the story. As to a second reason why Abraham refused the rich man's request, Arndt and Gingrich argue that the beginning of verse 26 should be translated, 'because of all these things', referring to the rich man's relationship on earth with Lazarus. Since the rich man did not bridge the chasm by helping Lazarus during his lifetime, Lazarus is unable to cross the chasm after death (Green, 1997).

The rich man had an obligation to help Lazarus both as one of the covenant people and also as his brother's keeper. P. R. Jones (1982) draws out two messages from the story: that existentially the insensitivity to someone's need through being self-centred shows an inauthentic existence, and that ethically one needs to keep the evangelical and social gospels together. Adewale sees implications from three perspectives for the African church. First, that globally with 250 million people in sub-Saharan Africa living on one dollar a day Christians in developed countries cannot ignore their distressed brothers and sisters. Second, that continentally the African church needs to get involved with the daily pain and struggles of people and not only be concerned about their souls. Third, locally rich African church ministers and members need to share with poor people in their area.

The story of the Rich Man and Lazarus needs to be read in conjunction with the rest of New Testament teaching, for example, about the basis on which God welcomes people into heaven. For example,

. repentance must include restoration of material resources to those who do not have them, in a levelling of the mountains and the valleys (Luke 3: 4-14);

. God's acceptance depends on how people have treated Christ in this life, based on how they have treated the least of Christ's brothers and sisters (Matt. 25: 31-46);

. more generally, God's acceptance is based not so much on a mental assent to a promise of salvation, but on evidence of how people obeyed God's Word and served their neighbour in this life, both these actions being in demonstration of their faith in Christ (e.g. Matt. 5-7, especially 7: 21-23; Luke 10: 25-37; Gal. 4: 14; James 2: 26);

. entrance into eternal life depends on whether we have put stumbling blocks in the way of the people Jesus considers 'little ones' (Matt. 18: 1-14);

. if our brother or sister has something against us we need to settle matters with them, otherwise we will need to pay the last penny (Matt. 5: 23-26).

In view of all this, the question that I think people need to grapple with is, 'How practically can rich white Christians get into heaven?' Does it mean that putting more money in the charity envelope fixes things with God? In the rest of this book I will try to explain what white Christians might need to do.

God uses the poor to bring in the harvest
Dana Jones (1987) captures the feelings of guilt and helplessness of rich white missionaries in the face of poverty. Dana was the daughter of missionaries who had returned to the United States. She went back at age 16 to try to renew contact in Mexico City with Celia, her closest Mexican friend.

'As we rounded a curve in the road, I spotted Celia's house and my heart sank. The entire house was the size of my bedroom. The walls were made of cariso (a type of wild cane that resembles bamboo) and held together with strips of tree bark. The roof was thatched with maguey plant leaves and an old beer crate served as the door.

I approached the dark little doorway and called Celia's name. In a few seconds she emerged. I had grown so much in the years since I had seen her that I towered above her now and had to bend down to hug her. She was a little shy, but was glad to see me. Her eyes looked tired, and her shoulders sagged. I heard a baby cry inside and she went back in to see what was the matter.

I ducked my head and started to follow Celia until something made me change my mind. When my eyes adjusted to the semi-darkness, I could make out her husband lying on a straw mat on the dirt floor ... obviously drunk. The smell of cactus liquor permeated the air. I quickly stepped back out into the sunlight and stood there blinking and feeling embarrassed. Then, Celia reappeared, carrying her baby son.

His little nose was streaming, and she wiped at it with her blouse. His diapers consisted of a strip of a cast-off shirt. Not that Celia wasn't a good mother, but being clean was a luxury for her family. The closest well was half a mile away and the water had to be carried in buckets. She offered me her only little chair, but I insisted she use it instead. My heart went out to Celia as I realized how our differences had become so obvious over the years. Her life had become so desolate and mine so full of potential....

Suddenly, my perspective was changed. I realized how blessed I was and how thankful I should be. I thanked God for education, for good nutrition, health, clothing and for living in America....

I deeply wanted to help Celia, but I felt powerless. I turned and looked at Diago, my little guide, and wondered what his life would be like. Then I realized that God could help me to make a difference. More than anything, these people needed the hope that God can give them and I want to deliver this message to people like Celia....

Knowing Christ may not improve living conditions for this group of people, but Jesus can surely help them through difficult times and help them rise above their circumstances....

The next morning, I took a bag of baby clothes to Celia's house. No one was home, but I left them there – along with a promise'.

Bonk admits that the Christian people who are 'reaching the unreached' are not in fact, primarily, the white missionaries. Rather, it is those who are referred to as 'national evangelists', who are living at the same level as the people and incarnate Jesus' message to them.

Missionary affluence was seen as an issue, for example, in China before the Cultural Revolution (Sung, 1995). For a Latin American critique of missionary affluence, see Orlando Costas (1973).

Conclusions

White Christians are complicit in a system as a result of which they are part of the global rich and have a luxurious daily lifestyle as a result of gaining daily the wealth of African, Asian and Latin American peoples. White Christians need to stand before God and ask how they need to change their lifestyles. According to the story of the rich man and Lazarus this is a matter of life and death. If rich white people do not bridge the chasm with oppressed, Majority World people in this world, there will be no way to bridge the chasm between heaven and hell in the next life.

According to Orlando Costas, their first responsibility is to show their lifestyle change towards Majority World people in their own country. As we will see, this is not, primarily, through individual repentance but through struggle with Majority World people to dismantle institutional racism in every area of society in each country, e.g. in education, employment, health, housing, social services, police, criminal justice, immigration, environment, politics and media (Kivel, 2011; Black Manifesto, 2010). Those looking for further reading might start with Beckford (1998). Perhaps the area in which they have the greatest chance to effect change is in the church, though this is easier said than done.

The implication of this is that white evangelicals need to change their priorities. Currently, top priorities for ministers and mission agencies and high priorities for church members are evangelism and discipleship. While we do not want to forget about the importance of these things, other things need doing first.

The greed, injustice, racism and domination that have fuelled present day inequality between the West and Majority World people not only threaten the likelihood of professing white Christians entering heaven, but also cause unreached peoples groups to reject the good news of Jesus that white Christians bring them. They are also turning postmodern young people away from the ways of their modern parents towards Majority World cultures and faiths. William H. Myers (2007) says that this blind spot regarding bad actions results from the Western church emphasizing orthodoxy (right doctrine) but de-emphasizing orthopraxis (right action).

Before doing anything else, there needs to be a process of repentance, restitution and reparations (Luke 3: 3-19; Matt. 5: 23-26; 7: 1-5). Without this there is no point in doing all the other good things people may have in mind.

The process of repentance, restitution and reparations needs to link in with a wider process of racial reconciliation. George Yancey (1998) explains four steps that have been used:

. Develop relationships with people of a different ethnic background from yourself. This introduces white people to a Britain as seen through the lives and eyes of those who experience its injustice.

. Recognise the social structures of inequality and recognize all Christians need to resist them together. Social structures include inequalities in areas such as education, housing, employment, etc. Doing nothing is the sin of indifference.

. White people, who have developed and benefited from a racialised society, need to repent of their historical, personal and social sins.

. African, Asian and Latin American people need to forgive whites corporately and individually, when they ask.

John Perkins saw that this message of reconciliation (Eph. 2: 11-22; 2 Cor. 5: 11-21) had been replaced with church growth. For Perkins, this was reproducing the church but losing the message (Perkins and Rice, 1993).

Part Two – The Bible as seen from the underside of history

Chapter 6
The Bible doctrine of oppression

'The besetting sins of the Anglo-Saxon race are the love of gain and the love of power,' Henry Highland Garnet (Fredrickson, 1995).

'"Honey, white man is de ruler of everything as fur as Ah been able tuh find out... So de white man throw down de load and tell de nigger man tuh pick it up. He pick it up because he have to, but he don't tote (carry, ed.) it. He hand it to his womenfolks. De nigger woman is de mule of de world so fur as Ah can see. Ah been prayin' fuh it tuh be different wid you. Lawd, Lawd, Lawd!"' (Hurston, 1937).

'People live in two different worlds. "You live in the world of the birds of the air, and we, in that of the fishes of the sea". Birds move fast, "because they fly. When we fishes move, we move relatively slower because we have to swim in an ocean ... of usury, tenancy and other unjust forces"' (Mang Juan, 1976).

Introduction

Here I show that oppression is the main cause of poverty in the OT. Over 60% of Israel's existence to the 2nd century CE was spent being oppressed by other nations. Oppression also exists within countries. The Messiah is prophesied to bring liberation from oppression. God's word to oppressors is, 'Let my people go!'

Many white people, who are advantaged under the current system of globalization, interpret and apply the Bible in a way that supports the status quo, how things are done at present under the system of globalization. Many Black, Asian and Latin American people, who are disadvantaged under the system of globalization, interpret and apply the Bible in a way that works to radically change this current system through liberation from their oppression. This demonstrates that Bible interpretation and application really is affected by your socio-economic experience in life. Two areas that show the difference of thinking between oppressors and the oppressed are the Bible doctrines of oppression and justice.

The doctrine of oppression

Hanks (1984) says the first occurrence in the Bible of a Hebrew word for oppression is in the Abrahamic covenant in Gen. 15: 13-14.

'Know thou beforehand that thy seed shall be a stranger in a land not their own, and shall bring them under bondage, and afflict (*'anah*) them four hundred years. But I will judge the nation which they shall serve, and after this they shall come out (liberation) with great substance'.

The experience of the Hebrews, similar to that of Joseph, looks forward to the Messiah's humiliation and exaltation. The experience is a typical one: immigrants without land, who are then enslaved; subsequently oppressed and suffering like beasts of burden. Liberation from oppression is therefore a fundamental provision, together with 'seed' and land, of the covenant with Abraham. Paul treats the Abrahamic covenant as the eternal covenant in Gal. 3 and 4. This must therefore inform our understanding of salvation to be integral liberation.

If the question was asked, 'What is the most important theme in the Old Testament?' perhaps there would be many different answers. A popular answer in the West would be the prophetic theme of the coming Messiah. We will return to this theme a bit later. One major aspect of the Old Testament, which also engages with the theme of prophecy of the coming Messiah, is that of the Exodus. Historically the period was long in comparison with much of Old Testament history: 430 years plus 40 years in the wilderness. Prophetically, it saw the fulfillment of the covenant promises to Abraham, in terms of the land and becoming a great nation (Gen. 12: 1-2). It also saw the production of the first five books of the Old Testament, the development of the law and the sacrifices that were to find their fulfillment in the self-sacrifice of the coming Messiah. The Israelites' faith was strengthened as they looked back at how God had delivered them and knew what God's expectations of them were so that they might avoid being sent into exile.

Who do you identify with as you read the Bible? Many white men may find it easiest to identify with the main person that a part of the Bible seems to be built around: Abraham, Moses, Samuel, the kings, Jesus, Paul. This is similar to white versions of history: history is viewed by 'winners' as the story of the 'winners'. White women often seem to focus on women: Sarah, Miriam, Ruth, Hannah, Mary, Elizabeth. Majority World people tend to focus on people who were in similar situations to their own, for example, Lot, Hagar, Joseph, the Hebrew midwives, Esther, ordinary people that Jesus met. The Exodus is very important to them.

As we look more closely at the Exodus, particularly at some excerpts such as Exodus 1: 8-14; 2: 23-25; and 3:7-10, some unexpected discoveries can be made.

First, there is a class struggle going on. This is a struggle of owners and workers, but more than that, of masters and chattel slaves, of oppressors and oppressed people. If we are middle class we might not recognize class struggle, but working class people certainly do, because they lose out as a result of it. We need to recognize the different classes because they are part of the story.

Then, God knows about the struggle. Even if we cannot see that there is a struggle going on between two different classes, God can. But God does more.

Further, God reacts to the struggle by taking sides. God shows that God is on the side of oppressed peoples and against oppressors (e.g. Ps. 9, 10; 72: 1-4).

Finally, God tells people to get involved in the struggle. While an obvious example is Moses leading the people, the people also needed to be involved in their liberation. So, for example, the believing Hebrew midwives ignored Pharaoh's orders and outwitted him, as a result of which God blessed them. A challenge here is to empower poor people to take action in their own liberation, rather than to take charge and try to do things for them, thereby disempowering them (Brown, 1984).

In the wilderness God gives laws in the 'Book of the Covenant' (Exod. 20:22 – 23: 33), part of which reads,

'Thou shalt not molest *(yanah)* a stranger, nor afflict *(lahats)* him: for yourselves also were strangers in the land of Egypt. You shall not hurt *('anah)* a widow or an orphan. If you hurt *('anah)* them they will cry out to me, and I will hear their cry: and my rage shall be enkindled, and I will strike you with the sword, and your wives shall be widows, and your children fatherless' (Exod. 22: 21-24).

Only in this place in the 'Book of the Covenant' does God say that God's anger threatens the guilty people. Only when people oppress the poor does the death penalty express God's anger.

Following Gerhard von Rad (1966), theologians have identified Deut. 26: 5-9 as a type of 'Apostles Creed' that Israelites confessed annually at the Feast of the First Fruits (similar to the way North America celebrates Thanksgiving Day). This celebrates the Exodus. It also means that the only cause of poverty that Israelites had to confess annually was oppression. The confession was:

'The Syrian pursued my father, who went down into Egypt, and sojourned there in a very small number, and grew into a nation great and strong and of an infinite multitude. And the Egyptians afflicted us, and persecuted *('anah)* us, laying on us most grievous burdens: and we cried to the Lord God of our fathers: who heard us, and looked down upon our affliction *('ani)*, our labour and distress *(lahats)*: and brought us out of Egypt with a strong hand, and a stretched out arm, with great terror, with signs and wonders: and brought us into this place, and gave us this land flowing with milk and honey'.

This passage teaches us a lot. First, there are in total ten basic Hebrew roots that usually mean the English word 'oppression' (see Table 8 below) according to major lexicons (e.g. Koehler and Baumgartner, 1958; Brown, Driver and Briggs, 1907; Holladay, 1971). These roots occur 525 times in the OT. They have different shades of meaning. They may also not be translated as 'oppression' by translators. Then again, different words for oppression may be used in the same text, highlighting different elements of the oppression. For example, *'anah* refers to the psychological effects of oppression, such as humiliation; *lahats* literally means to press or squeeze. Further, on 164 occasions in the Old Testament a word for oppression occurs in the same context as poverty. It is partly for this reason that oppression can be seen to be the main cause of poverty, which is why people are poor according to the Old Testament. In this passage the word for poverty is *'ani*. Finally, in addition there are a further ten Hebrew roots that are used less frequently (30 times) that according to the lexicons of Koehler and Holladay also usually mean 'oppression'.

In addition to these 555 occurrences of roots lexically defined, at some level, as 'oppression' in the OT there are other words, or metaphors, that while not usually meaning 'oppression' are used to indicate oppression. Looking at the prophet Amos, there are just two roots for oppression used with the poor: *'ashaq* with *dal* (in Amos 4:1b) and *ratsats* with *'ebyon* (4:1c). We might also compare *tsarar* used with *tsadiq*, or 'the just (5:12c). However, there are seven other instances where the prophet uses a word metaphorically for oppression and also linked to the poor:

'He hath sold the just man for silver,
and the poor *('ebyon)* man for a pair of shoes'. 2:6cd
'They bruise *(shwf)* the heads of the poor *(dal)*
on the dust of the earth,
and turn aside *(nth)* the way of the humble' *('anaw)*. 2:7ab
'Therefore because you robbed *(bshs)* the poor *(dal)*:
and took the choice prey from him:' 5:11ab
'and oppressing *(nth)* the poor *('ebyon)* in the gate'. 5:12d
'You who crush *(sh'f)* the poor *('ebyon)*,
and make the needy *('anaw)* of the land to fail' *(shbt)*. 8:4ab
'We may possess the needy *(dal)* for money
and the poor *('ebyon)* for a pair of shoes'. 8:6ab

If people were to study these metaphorical words for oppression they might double the number of O.T. verses that link oppression to poverty (Hanks, 1984).

Characteristics of oppressors and oppressed people

Elsa Tamez (2006) says three characteristics are common to oppressors.

Oppressors are trying to get more wealthy. 'And they have coveted fields, and taken them by violence, and houses they have forcibly taken away: and oppressed a man and his house, a man and his inheritance' (Mic. 2: 2). Accumulation of wealth for itself is wrong, since it results in despoiling others. God is against hoarding, so, 'O thou that dwellest upon many waters, rich in treasures, thy end is come for thy entire destruction' (Jer. 51: 13).

Again, oppressors have the mastery because they belong to the privileged or governing class. 'Woe to you that devise that which is unprofitable, and work evil in your beds: in the morning light they execute it, because their hand is against God' (Mic. 2: 1). 'Hear O ye princes of Jacob, and ye chiefs of the house of Israel: you that hate good and love evil...and have flayed (my people's) skin from off them: and have broken, and chopped their bones as for the kettle, and as flesh in the midst of the pot' (Mic. 3: 1-3).

Also, oppressors are idolaters. In each text mentioning oppression, there is a mention of contempt for God or a mention of idols. '(T)he house of Jacob ... are filled as in times past, and have had soothsayers…. Their land is filled with silver and gold: and there is no end of their treasures…. The land also is full of idols: they have adored the work of their own hands' (Is. 2: 6-8). Note the strong connection between accumulation of wealth and idolatry. When Jesus says that people cannot serve God and mammon (Matt. 6: 24), Raul Vidales (1978) says, 'Jesus… personifies money as a "false god". He is in fact condemning a concrete phenomenon: the accumulation of wealth by injustice and violence'.

Jose Porfirio Miranda (1982) says perfection of a culture of injustice happens when injustice is so deep rooted in oppressors that they don't realize they are guilty.

Oppressed people often trust in God. 'Why do you consume *(daka')* my people, and grind the faces of the poor *('ani)'*? (Is. 3: 15)

People are oppressed as a result of their being poor: they are also poor as a result of being oppressed. While 'poor' and 'oppressed' are synonyms, so are 'rich' and 'oppressors'. Yet God gives both oppressors and the poor the chance to work together for a fair society (Prov. 29: 13). Oppression is actually aimed against God: God is oppressed. 'He that oppresseth *('ashaq)* the poor, upbraideth his Maker: but he that hath pity on the poor honoureth him' (Prov. 14: 31). Similarly, the rejection of God's 'least', who are also 'the poor', in Matt. 25: 31-46, means rejecting God.

Methods of oppression

Elsa Tamez says that the top priority of oppressors is to increase their wealth at whatever cost. Impoverishment or death for the oppressed is only a secondary result. Religious, ideological and economic methods interact together in oppressors achieving their goal. Tamez separates the methods between those of foreign countries that oppressed Israel at the international level and the methods used by Israel to oppress their own people at the national level. We need to make the links here to our day, where on the one hand we see international companies and governments oppressing Majority World countries and on the other hand within each Majority World country, an elite group of landowners, shareholders and politicians who are nationals of that country, and whose power and lifestyle are maintained through their relationships with the international companies and states.

Eight methods of oppression were used during the history of Israel and Judah at the international level (see Table 7 below).

First, was enslavement and exploitation of workers. The Exodus story gives the best treatment of the oppression that Israel suffered. 'Therefore he set over them masters of the works, to afflict them with burdens, and they built for Pharaoh cities of tabernacles, Phithom and Rameses. But the more they oppressed them, the more they were multiplied and increased: and the Egyptians hated the children of Israel, and afflicted them and mocked them' (Exod. 1: 11-13).

Then, genocide. '"When you do the office of midwives to the Hebrew women", he said, "If it be a man child, kill it: if a woman, keep it alive"' (Exod. 1: 16). 'Pharaoh therefore charged all his people, saying, "Whatsoever shall be born of the male sex, ye shall cast into the river: whatsoever of the female, ye shall save alive"' (1: 22).

Also, there was the myth of idleness. '"Why do you Moses and Aaron draw off the people from their works? Get you gone to your burdens... how much more if you give them rest from their works?"' (Exod. 5: 4-5). '"They are lazy, and that is why their cry is, 'Let us go and sacrifice to our God'"' (Exod. 5:8). 'You are idle and therefore you say, "Let us go and sacrifice to the Lord". Go therefore and work: straw shall not be given you, and you shall deliver the accustomed number of bricks' (Exod. 5: 17-18). The Hebrews were hated because they wanted to be free (5: 22-23).

Again, there were deceitful concessions. Pharaoh granted peripheral requests, but only because he intended to keep oppressing and not grant complete freedom. So he says they can sacrifice to God 'in this land' (8: 25); 'but go no farther' (8: 28); 'but go ye men only' (10: 11); 'let your sheep only, and herds remain' (10: 24). If the Hebrews had accepted Pharaoh's offers, there would have been no radical struggle and no freedom for the Hebrews.

Also, there were unequal forces meeting together (Judges), 'The children of Israel cried to the Lord: for (Jabin) had nine hundred chariots set with scythes, and for twenty years had grievously oppressed (*lahats*, crushed) them' (Judg. 4: 3).

Further, there were plunder and slaughter. This was foretold in the Covenant Code as a punishment for not obeying God (Deut. 28: 33). For example, 'When Israel had sown, Midian, ... pitching their tents among them, wasted all things as they were in the blade ... they left nothing at all in Israel for sustenance of life, nor sheep, nor oxen, nor asses. For they and all their flocks came with their tents, and like locusts filled all places, an innumerable multitude of men, and of camels, wasting whatsoever they touched. And Israel was humbled exceedingly in the sight of Midian. And (Israel) cried to the Lord' (Judg. 6: 3-7).

Again, imposition of tribute or taxation. '(T)he King of the Assyrians put a tax upon Hezekiah, King of Judah, of three hundred talents of silver, and thirty talents of gold'. (2 Kings 18: 14b). Israel also exacted tribute from other nations (2 Sam. 8: 2).

Finally, exile. The dominated nation is either taken into exile or the dominators occupy them or appoint their rulers. 'Thus saith the Lord of hosts, "The children of Israel, and the children of Judah are oppressed (*'ashaq*) together: all that have taken them captives, hold them fast, they will not let them go' (Jer. 50: 33). In the "Oracles to the Nations", Is. 13-23, these foreign nations are called proud and arrogant. God says God will humble them when God avenges the oppressed (Is. 25: 5).

At the national level, there are seven methods of oppression. One example of these methods was the taking of Naboth's vineyard (1 Kings 21). Often, oppressors want more wealth; they are powerful and have nobles with them; they are idolatrous (21: 26); they use their power, false testimony and murder. As a general rule, oppressors invert values: they love evil and hate good (Is. 5: 20). When the Messiah comes, Isaiah says, 'Behold a king shall reign in justice, and princes shall rule in judgment.... The fool shall no longer be called prince: neither shall the deceitful be called great' (Is. 32: 1, 5). There will be justice for the oppressed.

The first method of oppression at the national level was exploitation of workers. The day labourers are required to work excessively and then are not paid. 'Woe to him that buildeth up his house by injustice, and his chambers not in judgment: that will oppress his friend without cause, and will not pay him his wages' (Jer. 22: 13). Slaves were not meant to be taken advantage of, or agreements reached with their former owners (Deut. 23: 15-16). Foreigners were supposed to be treated like nationals (Lev. 19: 33-34), but were commonly oppressed (Ezek. 22: 7).

Then, fraud, carried out either with unjust scales or through deceitful transactions. '(T)here is a deceitful balance in his hand, he has loved oppression. And Ephraim said, '"But yet I am become rich, I have found me an idol: all my labours shall not find me the iniquity that I have committed"' (Hos. 12: 7-8). 'And they have coveted fields, and taken them by violence, and houses they have forcibly taken away: and oppressed a man and his house, a man and his inheritance' (Mic. 2: 2).

Also, usury. '(He) grieveth the needy and the poor. (He) giveth upon usury and ... taketh an increase' (Ezek. 18: 12-13). This passage also challenges taking poor people's goods as pledges for their repayment of a debt.

Again, bribery. This takes place when judges take sides against the poor. 'Thy princes are faithless, companions of thieves: they all love bribes, they run after rewards' (Is. 1: 23).

Then again, being two-faced. Often, oppressors pretend to be friends. 'His words are smoother than oil, and the same are darts' (Ps. 55: 21).

Also, murder. 'Thy people, O Lord, they have brought low *(daka')*: and they have afflicted *('anah)* thy inheritance. They have slain the widow and the stranger: and they have murdered the fatherless' (Ps. 94: 5, 6).

Finally, they violate women using their strength. This is the only form of oppression not directly related to accumulation of wealth. 'They have discovered the nakedness of their father in (Jerusalem); they have uncovered the uncleanness of the menstruous woman. And everyone has committed abomination with his neighbour's wife, and the father-in-law has wickedly defiled his daughter-in-law, the brother has oppressed his sister the daughter of his father' (Ezek. 22: 10-11).

The Bible tells us that oppressors will be punished. God will take vengeance on them. Judah and Israel were punished by other nations.

The ministry of the coming Messiah, seen from Old Testament prophecies
When we look at the Old Testament prophecies of the coming Messiah we see much of the Messiah's concern to enable people to be freed from oppression. Psalm 72 is a Messianic psalm:

'Give to the king thy judgment, O God:
and to the king's son thy justice:
to judge thy people with justice,
and thy poor with judgment.
Let the mountains receive peace for the people:
and the hills justice.
He shall judge the poor of the people,
and he shall save the children of the poor: *('ebyon)*
and he shall humble the oppressor *('ashaq)....*
For he shall deliver the poor from the mighty:
and the needy *('ani)* that had no helper.
He shall spare the poor *(dal)* and needy:
and he shall save the souls of the poor.
He shall redeem their souls from usuries *(tok)* and iniquity (*hamas*):
and their names shall be honourable in his sight'. (Ps. 72: 1-4; 12-14).

The use of three words for poor a total of eight times in this passage and of two words for oppression shows how important liberation of poor people from oppression is to the ministry of the coming Messiah.

There are several prophecies in Isaiah about the birth of the Messiah. One is in Isaiah 8. 21- 9. 6. The context is of the Assyrian Empire annexing the north and east of Israel (subsequently Galilee of the Gentiles) in 734-732 BCE. Under terrible siege conditions, Judah was tempted to turn to spiritism for help (Is. 8: 19-20).

'And they shall pass by it, they shall fall *(qshh)* and be hungry:
And when they shall be hungry, they will be angry,
and curse their king, and their God, and look upwards.
And they shall look to the earth, and behold trouble *(tsarah)*
and darkness, weakness and distress *(tsuqah),* and a mist following them,
and they cannot fly away from their distress *(mutsaq)....*

For the yoke of their burden, and the rod of their shoulder, the sceptre of their oppressor *(nagas)* thou hast overcome as in the day of Midian.
For a child is born to us, and a son is given to us,
and the government is upon his shoulder:
and his name shall be called,
"Wonderful, Counsellor, God the Mighty,
the Father of the world to come, the Prince of Peace"'. (Is. 8:21, 22; 9: 4, 6).

There are five words in this passage that lexicons give the usual meaning of 'oppression'. Oppression is symbolised by the shadow of death and by darkness and gloom a total of six times (8: 22; 9: 1, 2). The liberation that comes with the Messiah's birth is one of light and joy like celebrating harvest time. Another symbol of oppression is the yoke and bar of oppressors. As every ox is beaten, so Assyria's treatment of Judah is like a farmer beating a cow with a rod. Celebration of liberation from this oppression is like the celebration of the victory of Gideon over the Midianites.

The coming of the Messiah is powerfully linked to these verses through the use of "because"/"for" (in Hebrew *ki* in verses 3, 4 and 5). So it is the *birth* of the Messiah, not only his second coming, which brings an end to oppression. So Luke shows this breaking of oppression in the hailing of Jesus' birth, including the political dimension (Luke 1: 32, 33, 51-54, 68-79). E. J. Young (1971) says, 'Salvation in its widest sense ('integral liberation?') had shined upon these people; a complete reversal of their condition had occurred'. Further, he says, 'The kingdom of the Son continually progresses. Justice and righteousness are its foundation; oppression and injustice have no part in its progress and growth'.

A prophecy of the wider ministry of the Messiah comes in Isaiah 42:1-4:

'Behold my servant, I will uphold him:
my elect, my soul delighteth in him.
I have given my Spirit upon him,
he shall bring forth judgment to the Gentiles.
He shall not cry,nor have respect to person,
neither shall his voice be heard abroad.
The bruised *(ratsats)* reed he shall not break,
and smoking flax he shall not quench:
he shall bring forth judgment unto truth.
He shall not be sad, nor troublesome *(ratsats)*,
till he set judgment in the earth:
and the islands shall wait for his law' (Is. 42:1-4).

E. J. Young sees the reed as the weak of any nationality. Being crushed (the literal meaning of *ratsats*) shows the nature of their oppression. According to Hebrew poetic parallelism, the wick similarly refers to oppressed peoples of all nations. This interpretation is supported by the facts that *ratsats* indicates a crushing form of oppression, that three times the servant is said to come to bring the justice that had been lacking (vv. 1, 3, 4) and by parallel references in other parts of Isaiah that indicate the work of the Messiah that brings justice to oppressed and poor people (e.g. Is. 11: 3-5; 58: 6). Further, in the same way that God's liberation in the exodus is not only for the Israelites but is a paradigm for God's work among all nations (Ps. 103: 6, 7, 17, 19), so the demonstration of the Spirit's baptism in and through the Messiah's ministry shown here in Isaiah is in bringing justice to the oppressed and poor of all nations (Is. 42: 1, 3, 4; c.f. 11: 2-5; 61: 1-2).

Arguably the most striking prophecy of the Messiah is that found in Isaiah 52: 13 - 53:12, the fourth Servant Song.

'Behold my servant shall understand,
he shall be exalted, and extolled, and shall be exceeding high.
As many have been astonished at thee,
so shall his visage be inglorious among men,
and his form among the sons of men.
He shall sprinkle many nations,
kings shall shut their mouth at him:
for they to whom it was not told of him, have seen:
and they that heard not, have beheld.
Who hath believed our report?
and to whom is the arm of the Lord revealed?
And he shall grow up as a tender plant before him,
and as a root out of a thirsty ground:
there is no beauty in him, nor comeliness: and we have seen him,
and there was no sightliness, that we should be desirous of him:
despised, and the most abject of men,
a man of sorrows, and acquainted with infirmity:
and his look was as it were hidden and despised,
whereupon we esteemed him not.
Surely he hath borne our infirmities
and carried our sorrows:
and we have thought him as it were a leper,
and as one struck by God and afflicted *('anah)*.
But he was wounded for our iniquities,
he was bruised *(daka')* for our sins:
the chastisement of our peace was upon him,
and by his bruises we are healed.
All we like sheep have gone astray,
every one hath turned aside into his own way:
and the Lord hath laid on him the iniquity of us all.
He was offered *(nagas)* because it was his own will *('anah),*
and he opened not his mouth:
he shall be led as a sheep to the slaughter,
and shall be dumb as a lamb before his shearer,
and he shall not open his mouth.
He was taken away from distress *('otser)* and from judgment:
who shall declare his generation?

because he is cut off out of the land of the living:
for the wickedness of my people have I struck him.
And he shall give the ungodly for his burial,
and the rich for his death:
because he hath done no iniquity,
neither was there deceit in his mouth.
    And the Lord was pleased to bruise *(daka')* him in infirmity:
if he shall lay down his life for sin,
he shall see his a long-lived seed,
and the will of the Lord shall be prosperous in his hand.
Because his soul hath laboured,
he shall see and be filled:
by his knowledge shall this my just servant justify many
and he shall bear their iniquities.
Therefore will I distribute to him very many,
and he shall divide the spoils of the strong,
because he hath delivered his soul unto death,
and was reputed with the wicked:
and he hath borne the sins of many,
and hath prayed for the transgressors'.

The traditional evangelical cessationist view of Isaiah 53 is that it maintains that the Messiah came to both provide a penal substitution and also forensic justification for believers. I support this view but do not believe that it exhausts all that the passage is saying about the Messiah. Just because one finds one subject in a passage does not rule out finding other important subjects in the same passage.

For example, we could consider a pentecostal interpretation which indicates that there is healing in the suffering of the Messiah. An alternative reading of verse 4a includes the words 'sickness' *(holi)* and 'pains' *(mac'ob)* .The Septuagint began the spiritualization by having, 'He bore our sins' *(hamartias)* but Matthew does not spiritualize when he says, 'He himself bore our sicknesses away and carried our diseases' (Matt. 8: 17). Words suggesting the Servant might have suffered from leprosy include *naga* (to touch, wound) in 53: 4c and *nega* (blow or plague) in 53: 8d. Is. 52: 14 and 53: 3, the latter saying 'one from whom, as it were, we averted our gaze', indicate that the Servant had a leprosy-like illness. 53: 10a says 'It was Yahweh's good pleasure to crush him with pain, or cause him to be sick': *(heheli)* is related to *holi* translated sickness in 3b and 4a. People's healing results from the Servant's sickness: 'and by his bruises we are healed *(rapha')' (53: 5b). So part of the Messiah's ministry is to heal people, as we read it is God who 'forgiveth all thy iniquities: who healeth all thy diseases' (Ps. 103:3).

If there is both healing and salvation in Is. 53, I suggest we also need to look closely at what is said in Is. 53 about oppression.

While the Servant is first seen alone in his exaltation (Is. 52: 13); by the end he shares the spoils of victory with his people (Is. 53: 12ab, cf. Luke 11: 22).

Four Hebrew roots meaning oppression are used six times in total. In 7a and 8a the Servant suffers oppression in the legal process. In 4b, 5d and 10a God wills the oppression, using sickness. The indifference of his own people (8b) may show that he was oppressed by a foreign power (7a, 8a). The revolution that brings liberation to the Servant (Is. 52: 13) happens in the context of the gentiles being afraid (52: 15a) and the kings being quiet (52: 15b). The Servant carries out God's just plans (53: 10d) and shares the spoils of the revolution with his followers, bringing liberation from oppression (53: 12ab). There are strong parallels between the Servant and Moses: the Israelites despoiled the Egyptians (Exod. 3: 21, 22).

The Servant suffers different kinds of oppression: psychological humiliation (Hebrew *'anah* vv. 4, 7); torture (*daka'* v. 5); degradation like an animal (*nagas* v. 7); injustice in a trial (*'otser* v. 8). Clearly oppression is a major theme in the central section, Is. 53: 4-10, yet commentators seem to ignore it.

The fourth Servant Song is placed immediately after the call for leaving Babylon and returning to Judea (Is. 52: 7-12). Liberation is not only from sin but from Babylonian oppression. Babylon had left Judea ecologically wasted and in drought. Pictures in Is. 40-55 confirm that liberation from oppression includes the return of a fertile land in place of ecological disaster.

So we find in Is. 53 a threefold picture of the coming Messiah: the one who brings salvation from sin, who brings healing and liberation from oppression. Hanks calls this Biblical salvation 'integral liberation'.

New Testament development of liberation from oppression

There are a range of continuities and discontinuities as we trace the theme of liberation from oppression in the New Testament. The Epistle of James is one of the continuities. James see class struggle as inevitable – 'Do not the rich oppress you by might *(katadunasteuo)*?' (2: 6b) - and that God's message is for the poor – 'hath not God chosen the poor in this world, rich in faith...?' (2: 5). Yet the impression given in Western theology is that it is the middle class that is elect, rather than the poor. James sees oppression as the main cause of poverty (2: 1-7 and 5: 1-6). The church both needs to care for its neediest members (2: 15-16) and needs to seek out the poor: God judges the church based on its orthopraxy, not on its orthodoxy.

'Religion clean and undefiled before God and the Father, is this: to visit the fatherless and widows in their tribulation *(thlipsis)*: and to keep one's self unspotted from this world.' (James 1: 27)

Recognising the teaching on praying for healing (5: 13-15) contributes to our understanding that salvation is integral, incorporating both physical healing and liberation from oppression as well as forgiveness of sin.

The most authoritative of Greek lexicons give oppression as the usual meaning of *thlipsis*, yet it never appears as oppression in the most common translations. Hanks (1984) produces a lot of evidence that both *thlipsis* and the verb *thlibo* should many times be translated 'oppression' or 'oppress' in the New Testament. Both words express causing socio-economic experience that translations such as 'affliction', 'suffering' and 'tribulation' suppress. So, for example, we read in Hebrews:

'But call to mind the former days, wherein, being illuminated, you endured a great fight of afflictions. And on the one hand, by reproaches and tribulations *(thlipsis)*, were made a gazingstock; and on the other, became companions of them that were used in such sort. For you both had compassion for them that were in bands, and took with joy the being stripped of your own goods, knowing that you have a better and a lasting substance'. (Heb. 10: 32-34).

The book of Hebrews may well have been written first to a group of converted priests (e.g. Acts 6: 7). On being baptized their public witness would have resulted in the loss of their property and inheritances through oppressive plundering. However, these priests looked ahead to the Final Judgment (10: 37) and stood in solidarity with Old Testament believers who were 'in want, distressed *(thlibo)*, afflicted' (11: 37). The class struggle of the Old Testament and James was still going on at the hands of the unconverted, rich oligarchy in Palestine. Similar uses of *thlibo* and *thlipsis* are in Matthew, Mark, Romans, 2 Corinthians, 1 and 2 Thessalonians and Revelation.

Luke-Acts and some discontinuities

One element of discontinuity with the Old Testament is that Luke avoids an obvious use of the word oppression so as to be sensitive to the handling of Luke-Acts in the Roman Empire. Instead the focus is on the Jewish religious oligarchy as the primary oppressors. Juan Luis Segundo (1976) indicates that their authority was political. Whereas we may think of a separation between the Romans as the state power and the Jewish authorities being 'the church', since first-century Palestine was a Judaistic theocracy, the state and the church were combined together and Jesus' teaching was a political threat, which was why he had to be eliminated.

The songs of Mary (Luke 1: 46-55) and Zechariah (1: 68-79) both attach the liberation theme to the birth of the Messiah:

'He hath put down the mighty from their seat, and hath exalted the humble.
He hath filled the hungry with good things; and the rich he hath sent empty away' (Luke 1: 52-53).

'Salvation from our enemies, and from the hand of all that hate us:
To perform mercy to our fathers, and to remember his holy testament …
that he would grant to us, that being delivered from the hands of our enemies,
we may serve him without fear.…

To enlighten them that sit in darkness, and in the shadow of death'. (1: 71-73b, 74a, 79a).

In Luke 4: 18-19 Jesus says his ministry is to poor and oppressed peoples. In the same way as Jesus said his was a ministry of fulfillment of the Old Testament, it also assumes, rather than attempts to prove, that oppression is the cause of poverty. Luke-Acts announces the coming of the solution to the problem of oppression and poverty.

'The Spirit of the Lord is upon me.
Wherefore he hath anointed me
to preach the gospel to the poor,
he hath sent me to heal the contrite of heart,
to preach deliverance to the captives,
and sight to the blind,
to set at liberty them that are bruised,
to preach the acceptable year of the Lord, and the day of reward'. (Luke 4: 18-19).

Jesus says that he has come to minister to a number of groups of people. First, to the poor. The word *ptochos* occurs 34 times in the NT, on all but one occasion meaning the materially poor. The materially poor were most of the people in first-century Palestine. Many were landless. To show his solidarity with them, he had just suffered hunger for forty days. But he also lived as a poor person and spoke to them 'from below' rather than 'from above'. Then, to the captives. Most prisoners in first century Palestine were executed rather than left in prison for long periods. Most that were in prison were there because they were debtors: they were imprisoned because they were poor. Also, to the oppressed. Oppression and injustice were the primary causes of poverty. Finally, to the blind. On six of the seven occasions when Luke mentions blind people, he also mentions their poverty. This also shows that a purpose of Jesus' healing ministry was to bring liberation from oppression.

Jesus quotes from Is. 61: 1-2. This refers clearly to the year of jubilee of Lev. 25. However, the interesting point is that Jesus includes a key liberative phrase, 'to set at liberty them that are bruised' which is not in Is. 61 but is a quotation from Is. 58: 6. Why is Jesus quoting from Is. 58 as well as from Is. 61? The link between the jubilee and Isaiah 58 is only just being recognized. The following provides some justification.

First, Is. 58 is part of a section from ch. 56 to ch. 58 on the Sabbath. The jubilee is a Sabbath year: teaching on the jubilee concludes (Lev. 26: 2) with an encouragement to keep the Sabbath similar to Is. 58: 13-14. Then again, the main theme of Is. 58 is the nature of true fasting. The only fast commanded in the law is the fast of the Day of Atonement (Lev. 16: 29-31). The year of jubilee began on that day of fasting (25: 9). The fast God chooses is that of the socio-economic revolution of the jubilee. Also, the year of jubilee is announced with the trumpet similarly to Is. 58: 1ab. This declares Jacob's (Israel's) sins (58: 1cd) of coveting and injustice.

Again, Isaiah 58: 2 refers to the forsaking of one of God's laws, leading to oppression and injustice. The jubilee was neglected. Also, the 'acceptable year' (mentioned both in the jubilee and in Is. 61: 2) was to be started with the 'acceptable day' of Is. 58: 5, also the fasting day of the Atonement.

'Is not this the fast that I have chosen?
Loose the bands of wickedness,
undo the bundles that oppress, let them that are broken go free,
and break asunder every burden.' (Is. 58: 6).

Further, the re-iteration of the freeing of slaves four times in Is. 58: 6, referring to Lev. 25: 8-55, leads Westermann (1969) to conclude that freedom from any sort of bondage is the emphasis. Also, the needs of some could not wait for the time of liberation. Is. 58: 7 relates to the provisions of the jubilee to take the homeless into your home and give food without charge (Lev. 25: 35-37). Again, while the jubilee calls for canceling debts (Lev. 25: 10; 35-55), striking with fists (Is. 58: 4) would seem to refer to debt collection incidents. Also, 'malicious words', Is. 58:9, for example Ahab's taking of Naboth's vineyard, is in contrast to restoring property rights to debtors. Finally, by quoting Is. 58: 6 as well as Is. 61: 1-2, Jesus is underlining the importance of liberation from oppression as part of the integral nature of the salvation he brings. The Sabbath is a weekly microcosm of the jubilee Sabbath year.

What Jesus had to say about Naaman and the widow of Zarephath made people realize that he was turning everything upside down. Their reaction was to try to kill him. Brown (1984) explains what Jesus was really saying.

'The land is not to be exploited any more, slaves are to be freed, debts are to be cancelled, capital unjustly gained is to be redistributed. Any political, economic, social or religious structures that perpetuate exploitation must be changed to create a society committed to the reversal of the plight of the poor (meaning the material poor), the captives (meaning the dregs), the blind (meaning the blind) and the oppressed (meaning the victims). The provisions of the jubilee are not spiritual consolation prizes for those who fail to make it here and now, they are specific descriptions of what the here and now is *already* in process of becoming'.

In Luke's story of the early church, Peter explains a discontinuity with the Old Testament.

'Jesus of Nazareth: (you know) how God anointed him with the Holy Ghost, and with power, who went about doing good, and healing all that were oppressed *(katadunasteuo)* by the devil, for God was with him' (Acts. 10: 38).

Peter says that what Jesus does is to heal the oppressed. So we can understand the healings of Luke-Acts as the liberation of oppressed people. The healings replace the plagues of the Exodus. The devil lies behind the power of the oppressors. Healing is a victory against the demonic spiritual power that lies behind the political dimension of oppression.

Hanks shows there are six cycles in Acts 1-12 of the same five elements; miraculous acts of liberation (mainly healings); the good news proclaimed to the poor; conflict with religious-political oppressors and witness to them; justice for the oppressed in the new community; expansion of the church (mainly poor people). E.g.

'First Cycle: 2: 1-47

1. The miracle of Pentecost, 1-13, 19.

2. Proclamation of the good news to the poor, 14-41, especially v. 18 (the Spirit given to the poor).

3. Denunciation of oppression, 23, 36, 40.

4. Justice for the poor of the new community, 42, 44-45.

5. Favour with the masses, 47a'.

The other cycles are Acts 3: 1 – 4: 37; 5: 1 – 6: 7; 6: 8 – 9: 42; 10: 1 – 11: 30; and 12: 1 – 16.

So in Acts 1-12 we have a focus on liberation of the oppressed and poor together with justice that they achieve within the church in Palestine. This focus acts as a departure point for sharing the good news with the poor and the growth of the church. The miracles, of liberating people and healing, bring confrontation with the religious-political oppressors as well as witness to them. These acts of liberation should be seen as signs that the messianic age has arrived, in which the oppressed and poor achieve justice. This fulfils Jesus' ministry plan of Luke 4: 18-19. There are similarities in these elements in Jesus' sending out of the twelve in Luke 9: 1-19, e.g.

1. The twelve sent out to heal and preach the kingdom, 9: 1-2.

2. They identify completely in their lifestyle with the poor, 9: 3-5.

3. Herod is provoked by hearing news of their miracles and proclamation, 9: 7-9.

In Acts 13-28 the miracles are seen in the form of the conversion of Gentiles. The oppression that Paul suffers is in the form of persecution: oppression results from greed, whereas persecution results from religious zeal. Persecution does not replace oppression: God's poor people are no longer only oppressed but persecuted as well. In Acts 13-28 we see oppression not seen primarily as sickness but as the result of the devil's activity that develops oppression through persecution. A useful way of understanding the relation of Paul's ministry among the Gentiles to Jesus' ministry is to compare Acts. 26: 17-18 to Luke 4: 18-19. This shows that far from Paul's work being a spiritualization of the gospel through ignoring the material, the emphasis is on seeing all oppression – tyranny, economic injustice, sickness – as under the devil's authority from which Jesus provides integral liberation. The oppressed poor enjoy liberation through the year of jubilee practiced within the community of the church which shows God's purposes for God's universal kingdom.

Pervasiveness of oppression – oppression of Israel in OT times

Table 7 Oppression of Israel/Judah in Old Testament times. (Source: biblehub.com).

```
O.T. chronology                                   Oppression of Israel/Judah

2091         Call of Abraham      2085-2067    Sodom (incl 4 kings)        18
                                  1929-1906    Esau + Laban                41
                                  1889-1886    Potiphar's wife + prison    44
                                  1600-1446    Enslavement in Egypt       198
1406         Cross Jordan         1406-1399    Canaanites                 205
1399-1049    Judges               1399-1391    Cushan                     213
                                  1351-1333    Eglon                      231
                                  1253-1233    Jabin                      251
                                  1193-1186    Midianites                 258
                                  1098-1080    Ammonites                  276
1075-1035    Samuel               1080-1050    Philistines                306
1045-1010    Saul                 1043-1042    Ammonites                  307
                                  1041-998     Philistines                350
1010-970     David                995-993      Ammon + Syria              352
970-930      Solomon              970-930      Edom + Syria               392
                                  930-908      Jeroboam (Israel)          414
                                  908-884      Baasha (Israel)            438
                                  857-853      Syria                      442
                                  852-850      Moab                       444
                                  840-790      Syria                      494
                                  751-632      Assyria                    613
                                  609-604      Egypt                      618
                                  604-538      Babylon                    684
                                  538-331      Persia                     891
                                  330-323      Greece                     898
                                  323-129      Ptolemaic+Seleucids       1092
                                  129-63       Seleucids                 1158
                                  63-136       Rome(to Judea exile)      1357

No. of years                      2227                                   1357
                                                                       (60.9%)
```

We have looked so far mainly at oppression from the perspective of the individual oppressed person, oppression at the grassroots level and seen that many Israelites were oppressed throughout much of their history. Oppression was also exerted at the national, institutional level. Another level is that of one nation oppressing another one, oppression at the international level (Tamez, 2006).

When we consider the oppression that Israel experienced at the international level, between the time of Abraham's call and the sending into exile by the Romans of people from Judea, we see that for over 60% of Israel's national lifetime in Bible times it was oppressed by other nations. This might not be so surprising when we consider the pervasiveness of oppression of individuals as the Bible records.

What we do need to consider seriously, therefore, is that the Bible is God's record of God's dealings with an in general oppressed people, where God intervenes throughout in the cause of oppressed people and, by implication, is against oppressors, in such a way as to be willing to kill oppressors (Ps. 72: 4).

From the evidence of the last several hundred years up to the present day, the nations that have been oppressing other nations internationally, through systems such as colonialism and globalization (Watkins and Shulman, 2010), would mainly seem to be those based in the West. God's message to oppressors in the Bible is not the same as God's message to oppressed peoples. God's word to oppressors is not 'share your faith with as many people as have never heard about Jesus'. God's words to oppressors start with the following: 'Let my people go!' (Exod. 5: 1).

This message comes to oppressors, the Egyptians, who are maintaining their inflated standard of living by inflicting enslavement on Israel. The picture is of the jubilee (Lev. 25). You have gained income for a number of years through the impoverishment of your own flesh and blood and God tells you that after 50 years that's enough and you need to set them free (Tan, 2008). In the New Testament John the Baptist brings a word of repentance to oppressors. His message to rich people, "Every valley shall be filled, and every mountain and hill shall be brought low" (Luke 3: 5) shows that repentance 'has as its core the obligation and duty to empower all to complete living' (Crowder, 2007).

As we shall see more in the next chapter, the approach of much of the Western church has been to focus on their repentance from sin against God and to rely on intellectual statements of their belief about God, that is, to focus on their vertical relationship with God, their theology. This has been at the expense of virtually ignoring their horizontal relationship with, and sin against, their fellow person, their 'neighbour', their ethics. When many people see Bible verses about the relationship with the neighbour, they can tend to spiritualize them into meaning relationships with fellow believers ('the righteous', see chs. 7, 8), hence less important than relationship with or sin against God. But God puts the relationships the other way round. 'If any man say, "I love God" and hateth his brother; he is a liar. For he that loveth not his brother, whom he seeth, how can he love God, whom he seeth not' (1 John 4: 20)? 'Thou shalt love the Lord thy God with thy whole heart... *and thy neighbour as thyself*' (Luke 10: 27). The Bible's focus from the beginning throughout Genesis has been on the relationship with the human brother and sister, believing or non-believing, whom you have seen as the way to demonstrate evidence that you are in a relationship with the God whom you have not seen. Alienation from our fellow humans results in alienation from God. We see the face of Christ in the alien and the hungry (Matt. 25: 35-6) (Amos, 2004). So sin is more what you do wrong to your neighbour, as well as what you do wrong towards God. Ubuntu, on the other hand, is a communal way of life, run for the benefit of everyone. It requires co-operation, charitableness and sharing (Paul, 2009).

Table 8 Vocabulary for oppression in relation to poverty in the Old Testament. Source: (Hanks, 1984).

Hebrew root	Meaning	Total OT occurrences	Occurrences with poverty in context
'shq	injustice	59	31
ynh	enslave	20	15
ngs	animalize	23	20
lhts	squeeze (pain)	31	17
rtsts	crush	20	9
dk'	pulverise	31	10
'nh	humiliate	82	14
"tsr, "tsrr	enmity	96	9
'tsrr, 'tsr, 'tsrh	impoverish	132	10
Tsuq + cognates	besiege	31	14
10 Less frequent Hebrew roots		30	15
Total 20 Hebrew roots, lexically defined as 'oppress', 'oppression', etc.		---	---
		555	164

Chapter 7
The Bible doctrine of justice - 1 Old Testament

'The issue (the ideological bias of translators) becomes readily apparent when one compares the most influential Bible translations for the English-speaking and Spanish-speaking worlds - the King James Version for the English-speaking world and the Reina Valera Revisada for the Spanish speaking world.... A computer search for the word justice in the KJV finds that it appears only 28 times in the entire Bible. A further interesting fact is that of those 28 uses of the term justice, none are to be found in the New Testament.... The same search carried out in the RVR reveals that the word justicia ("justice") appears a total of 370 times. The term can be found 101 times in the New Testament.... The term is used more than 13 times as often in the RVR as in the KJV.... A further comparison can be done by looking at the use of justice in other English... translations: KJV 28x; TEV 103x; ASV 116x; RSV 125x; NKJV 130x; NRSV 131x; NIV 134x; NAB 221x; NJB 253x.... This is further substantiated by a look at two standard translations in German and French. The Revised Martin Luther Text (1985) has the word gerechtigkeit ("justice") 306 times. The French Nouvelle Version Segond Révisée has justice 380 times, and the Latin Vulgate ... utilizes iustitia over 400 times' (Voth, 2003).

'From both sides within would-be Christian culture – those who deny the resurrection, and thereby cut off the branch from which true Christian work for justice must grow, and those who affirm (the resurrection) but use it to reinforce their anti-thisworldly theology – we find apparently powerful reasons for doing nothing about the plight of the world and for letting things take their own course, which means of course the strong go on winning. Implicit social Darwinism again' (Wright, 2011).

Introduction

I consider here Voth's comparison of the KJV and the Spanish RVR in how they generally translate *sedeq*. Voth shows how the context often determines that justice is a better translation than righteousness. He shows that it was not in James I's interests to have Puritans appealing to justice as the Bible saw it when James thought only the King should decide what justice was. I look at the views of Miranda, Gaebelein and Weinfeld on the usage and translations of *sedeq* and *mispat*.

Justice is seen by people of the Majority World as intrinsic to the gospel and therefore the goal of Christian living. Justice is grounded in the reality of marginalized and oppressed people, so justice is about liberative theological and ethical praxis that is aimed at doing away with oppression in relationships, in structures and in societies (Isasi-Diaz, 2000). In short, praxis is all of the human practices in the social realm.

The unmarked (default or usual) meaning of *sedeq*

Voth (2003), a Bible translator experienced in translating into Spanish, looks at the Hebrew word *sedeq* which occurs 119 times in the OT. The King James Version (KJV) translates *sedeq* as 'righteousness' 82 times, as 'righteous' 10 times and as 'right' 3 times. It does this even more so with other cognates of the root *s-d-q*, for example, the feminine noun *sedaqa* which occurs 157 times. Meanwhile the Reina Valera Revisada (RVR) consistently translates these as 'justice'. Having said this, *sedeq* and its cognates has a range of other meanings, dependent on context, including 'just' (e.g. weights in Pentateuch, ordinances in Psalms); right behaviour; a forensic sense (e.g. in Job arguing for his innocence); and God's saving action, in addition to 'justice'. *Sedeq* is often also used in conjunction with another noun or nouns, for example *mispat*, which together would usually mean 'social justice'.

Voth's analysis of the word 'righteousness' concludes that 'righteousness'
- Is not active but passive: it is a state of being, not becoming
- It is theologically bound: it refers to someone in right standing with God, so
- It is not secularly relevant: it doesn't engage with non-Christians' issues
- It is individualistic as opposed to community orientated. Community orientation in the Bible is often only seen by the translator rather than by the reader: for example, when commands in the original language are plural, they are addressed to the community, rather than to an individual.

We can deduce some things from history as to why the word 'righteousness' was preferred in the KJV. One guideline for the KJV translators was that the Bishops' Bible, at that time chained in Anglican churches, was to be followed and changed as little as possible. The Bishops' Bible never uses 'justice' to translate *sedeq*. Further, a word like 'justice' that spoke of a community demand would not sit well with James I, who laid claim to the divine right of kings and lived a luxurious lifestyle. However, using a word like 'righteousness', which reflected a common Puritan concern for individual holiness and piety, might fit the royal agenda well.

Voth analyses examples of *sedeq* in Deuteronomic, poetic and prophetic literature. He concludes that the primary meaning of *sedeq* should be 'justice'. He also makes two preliminary suggestions. First, there needs to be a move in the church away from the individualistic worldview that seems to be spreading from the West to other parts of the world. The church can make its first step towards de-privatising the faith by incorporating the communal challenge of biblical justice present in *sedeq* and its cognates. Change can then take place from people's passive state of being, where the focus is on a person's righteousness, to a more active communal concern for 'the Other', breaking down the separation between the spiritual and secular areas of life. This will enable the church to actively engage the world that is focused on thirsting for power with a relevant message of hope, based on thirsting for justice that comes out from the communities.

Voth's other suggestion is that the world's needs will be addressed far more effectively if the church understands the communal views of justice expressed by the *sedeq* word family. Faced by global injustice the church has too often expressed a righteous response of indifference based on a feeling that we can't solve all the world's problems. Privatised spirituality then focusses on individual righteousness and well-being. What the church needs instead is to take seriously the responsibility to be salt and light in the world, to show by interpreting *sedeq* more as 'justice' that everyone has the right to a life of respect and decency, so that the church declares genuine hope to the world. One obvious example is by developing a more just economic system than today's neo-liberal globalization.

Jose Porfirio Miranda (1982) explains how God engages in justice in the Bible. Miranda says that when Jeremiah challenges Shallum (Jehoahaz) about his lifestyle, he reminds him of his father Josiah when he says:

'Did not thy father eat and drink
and do judgment and justice,
and it was then well with him?
He judged the cause of the poor and needy
for his own good:
was it not therefore because he knew me,
saith the Lord?' (Jer. 22: 15b-16).

So to know the Lord is to do justice to the poor. Similarly, in Hosea we read:

'(T)here is no truth, and there is no mercy,
and there is no knowledge of God in the land.
Cursing, and lying, and killing, and theft,
and adultery have overflowed,
and blood hath touched blood' (Hos. 4:1b-2).

The opposing of 'knowledge of God' with inter-human crimes shows that 'knowledge of God' indicates justice among people. Hosea uses this formula of 'knowledge of God/the Lord' five times. The identification of knowing God with inter-human justice goes back to the 10th century BCE. Hosea speaks about people's cruel relationships:

'What shall I to do to thee, O Ephraim?
what shall I to do to thee, O Juda?
your mercy is as a morning cloud,
and as the dew that goeth away in the morning.
For this reason have I hewed them by the prophets,
I have slain them by the words of my mouth:
and thy judgments shall go forth as the light.

For I desired mercy, and not sacrifice:
and the knowledge of God more than holocausts' (Hos. 6: 4-6).

H. J. Kraus (1957) says that Isaiah, Hosea, Amos and Micah focus on one theme: 'justice and right'. G. J. Botterweck (1951) says that the Jeremiah 22 passage above shows what all the prophets see as knowing God: inter-human justice. H. W. Hertzberg (1923) perceptively comments, 'One impedes his own understanding if he thinks here of what we understand today as 'living and knowing God', that is, an activity between man and God'. His point is that we can only know God through our inter-human justice demonstrated towards other people.

Hosea 6:6 is quoted in Matt. 9: 13 and 12: 7, where *hesed* (KJV mercy in Hos. 6: 6) is understood as inter-human compassion (Septuagint *eleos* in Hos. 6:6). The synonymous parallelism between compassion and knowing God in Hos. 6:6 and their contrast with sacrifice and burnt offerings show that knowing God has regard to inter-human relationships.

Synonymous parallelism is a figure of speech used in Hebrew poetry: the words in the first line of a verse seem to be repeated very similarly in the second line of the verse. In synonymous parallelism, it would likely be a mistake to interpret colons or phrases as if they were communicating distinctly different meanings from each other.

Hesed does not mean a vertical 'religious' relationship with God, which rather is a case of Western spiritualization. *Hesed* appears in hendiadys or synonymous parallelism with right (*mispat*) or justice (*sedaqa*) in the following passages: Ps. 25: 8-9; 33: 5; 36: 5-6, 10; 40: 10; 85: 10; 88: 11-12; 89: 14; 98: 2-3; 103: 17; 119: 62-64; Is. 16: 5; Jer. 9: 24; Hos. 2: 19-20; 6: 5, 6; 10: 12; 12: 6; Mic. 6: 8; Zech. 7: 9. So, to know God means both having compassion for the poor and needy and doing justice to them. Hendiadys is the use of two nouns (for example, 'justice' and 'right') for greater effect on the reader, when the meaning is one of these nouns as an adjective modifying the other noun, in this example 'right justice' or 'social justice'.

In Hos. 2: 19-20 God betroths Israel in right and justice and in compassion so that they would know God. In Is. 11: 2d, 4 and 9 the Messiah shows his knowledge of the LORD by defending the poor with justice and the needy with equity. Hab. 2: 14 quotes Is. 11: 9, showing an overflowing of justice that ends Babylonian domination.

The prophets are agreed on the importance of worship compared with justice:
'I hate and have rejected your festivities:
and I will not receive the odour of your assemblies.
And if you offer me holocausts, and your gifts,
I will not receive them:
Neither will I regard
the vows of your fat beasts.
Take away from me the tumult of thy songs:

and I will not hear the canticles of thy harp.

But judgment shall be revealed as water,

and justice as a mighty torrent.

Did you offer victims and sacrifices to me

in the desert for forty years, O house of Israel?' (Amos 5: 21-25)

God indicates that God does not want worship: rather God wants inter-human justice. This distinguishes God from other gods. God says that to know God is to do right and justice and compassion to the needy. If we seek to know God directly in some other way, supposing that God is always there when we want God, at that point God is not God but an idol. The message is the same in Is. 1: 10-20 (note, prayer is rejected); 43: 23-24; 58: 2, 6-10; Jer. 6: 18-21; 7: 4-7; 11: 15, 21-22.

In Jeremiah we read the following about the priests' response to Josiah's reforms:

'Trust not in lying words, saying:

"The temple of the Lord, the temple of the Lord, it is the temple of the Lord".

For if you will order well your ways and your doings: if you will execute judgment between a man and his neighbour,

if you oppress not the stranger, the fatherless and the widow, and shed not innocent blood in this place,

and walk not after strange gods to your own hurt,

I will dwell with you in this place:

in the land which I gave to your fathers from the beginning and for evermore.

Behold, you put your trust in lying words….

Thus saith the Lord of hosts the God of Israel:

"Add your burnt offerings to your sacrifices, and eat ye the flesh.

For I spoke not to your fathers, and I commanded them not,

in the day that I brought them out of the land of Egypt,

concerning the matter of burnt offerings and sacrifices.

But this thing I commanded them, saying:

"Hearken to my voice, and I will be your God, and you shall be my people:

and walk ye in all the way that I have commanded you, that it may be well with you"'. (Jer. 7: 4-8, 21-23).

Worship and prayer cannot put us in contact with God while injustice remains on earth. The reform of Josiah was well-intentioned, but according to Jeremiah the priests and scribes were wrong in worshipping when justice had not yet been achieved (Jer. 7: 4-8, 21-23; 8: 8-12; 14: 11-16; 23: 25-29, etc.) (e.g. North, 1936). People are in this case worshipping a different god, because God says God is known as people do justice to the poor, or 'do justice and right injustice' (Wolterstorff, 2013).

While there is injustice among people worship does not have God as its object, but an idol. We can approach an idol directly: we can approach God when we are doing justice to the poor. People might then object, 'If we are to wait until justice is done in the earth we'll never worship God'. What they are saying is that they don't believe justice will ever be done on earth, because this is too difficult, and therefore they will not try to work hard for justice because it is time-wasting. The prophets, however, were convinced that justice could and must be realized on earth: they did not give up and say justice is impossible. Everything that they did and said results from the fact that they would not accept injustice just because achieving justice was too difficult. The prophets clearly believed in a time on earth when justice will be done and then people will worship God, e.g., Is. 2: 2-4; Ezek. 36: 24-38; Hos. 2: 21-25; 14: 2-3, Mic. 4: 1-8; Zeph. 3: 9-13; Zech. 5: 5-11.

God's Intervention

In Exod. 6: 2-7 we find that the way in which people will know the Lord is through God's work to bring out and free, with an outstretched arm and great judgments, God's oppressed people who cry out (3: 7-9) to God (6: 5 'groaning'). This way of knowing and understanding God continues through the Old Testament. In Is. 40-55, Westermann (1969), Zimmerli (1964) and Hertzberg (1922) see God intervening on behalf of the oppressed in destroying the Babylonian imperial domination (e.g. Is. 41: 17, 20, 27; 45: 13, 21, 24; 46: 12-13). Miranda notes synonymous parallelism between salvation and justice in Ps. 65: 5; 71: 15; 98: 2; Is. 45: 8, 21; 46: 13; 51: 5, 6, 8; 56: 1; 59: 17; 61: 10. God achieves faithful love, justice and uprightness on earth, according to Jer. 9: 24.

The Western theology of providence, inherited from the thinking of the Greeks, is static, non-specific and sees praiseworthy events as instants that are isolated points. For the Bible, however, God is the Creator and has a plan and intervenes in history in order to change the world so it can become a world of justice. So we find that Yahweh looks forward to bringing about justice worldwide (e.g. Is. 42: 1, 6; 45: 21-23; 49: 6; 51: 4-8; 54: 2-3; 55: 5).

God's Plan

In the first story of people outside the garden of Eden we hear, 'The voice of thy brother's blood crieth to me from the earth' (Gen. 4: 10). God hears the cry of the oppressed and responds to inter-human injustice with a curse on Cain. The first death in history results from oppression. The word 'brother' is repeated seven times and indicates the responsibility people have to be their brother's and sister's keeper.

In Gen. 18: 18-21 the outcry came to God about the oppression by wealthy Sodom of the needy (Is. 1: 10, 15, 17; Jer. 23: 14; Ezek. 16: 49). It is because God intervenes to heed oppressed people's cries that God shares God's plan for Sodom with Abraham, since God is using Abraham to bring justice and right (v. 19). In the Old Testament, the hendiadys 'justice and right' (*sedaqa umispat* or *mispat usedaqa*) appears 31 times (Gen. 18: 19; 2 Sam. 8: 15; 1 Kings 10: 9; 1 Chron. 18: 14; 2 Chron. 9: 8; Ps. 33: 5; 89: 14; 97: 2; 99: 4; 119: 121; Prov. 1: 3; 2: 9; 21: 3; Eccles. 5: 8; Is. 9: 7; 33: 5; Jer. 4: 2; 9: 24; 22: 3, 15; 23: 5; 33: 15; Ezek. 18: 5, 19, 21, 27; 33: 14, 16, 19; 45: 9; Hos. 2: 19). The two words are used in synonymous parallelism 23 times (Job 35: 2; 37: 23; Ps. 36: 6; 37: 6; 72: 1; 99: 4; 103: 6; 106: 3; Prov. 8: 20; 16: 8; Is. 1: 27; 5: 7, 16; 28: 17; 32: 16; 54: 17; 56: 1; 59: 9, 14; Amos 5: 7, 24; 6: 12; Mic. 7: 9). There are 11 other occurrences of the parallelism with *sedeq* in place of *sedaqa* (Deut. 16: 18; Job. 8: 3; 29: 14; Ps. 9: 4; 72: 2; 94: 15; Is. 1: 21; 16: 5; 26: 9; 32: 1; Jer. 22: 13). There are a further 32 occasions on which the roots *spht* and *sdq* are paired together (Lev. 19: 15; Deut. 1: 16; 16: 19; 25: 1; 1 Sam. 12: 7; 2 Sam 15: 4; 1 Kings 8: 32; 2 Chron. 6: 23; Job 9: 15; Ps. 7: 9, 11; 9: 4, 8; 35: 24; 50: 6; 51: 4; 58: 1, 11; 82: 3; 96: 13; 98: 9; Prov. 8: 16; 31: 9; Eccles. 3: 17; Is. 1: 26; 11: 4; 16: 5; 43: 26; 51: 5; 59: 4; Jer: 11: 20; Ezek. 23: 45).

A Jewish writer, Moshe Weinfeld (1992), confirms that the hendiadys, 'justice and right' could best be translated as 'social justice'. This hendiadys is not an ordinary one, owing to the number of cases of synonymous parallelism. In practice, the two terms are synonymous: one term might be used for the complete hendiadys. Evidence for this is seen in the Septuagint. *Sedaqa* is commonly translated as *dikaiosune* and *mispat* as a substantive derived from *krino* (*krima* or *krisis*). However, 48 times the translators choose *dikaiosune* as a translation of *mispat*, showing that they see *mispat* as synonymous with *sedaqa*.

Miranda has problems with the translation of *sedeq* in English versions as 'righteousness' instead of 'justice'. He says that use of the words 'the righteous' and 'the wicked', particularly in the Psalms, appeals to Western thinking, which tends to spiritualize the meaning of the Bible, particularly to avoid facing up to Western oppression of the poor and God's view of that oppression. It runs into problems in the Psalms, for example Psalm 37, which is clearly about oppression by the unjust (*resaim* v. 14). This characterization of the Psalms and the Bible as a battle between believers and unbelievers, that is between the good people (us) who have God on their side and the bad people ('the Other') who do not, maximizes the importance of spiritual poverty and ignores the predominance of material poverty in the Bible together with the fact that oppressors cause that material poverty

Further, Miranda says the use of 'righteousness' and 'righteous' is ideologically dangerous. Modern Western exegesis tends to split ethics from theology by emphasizing a spiritual relationship with God, the vertical relationship, at the expense of horizontal relationships in the material world with their neighbour, brother and sister. Sider (2008) speaks of the danger of limiting the words to 'personal relations and inner attitudes'. Righteousness can almost be interpreted as a 'feelgood factor' that justifies 'the way we live' rather than that showing that we are committed to working with God towards bringing in God's world of justice (Costas, 1989; Schrenk, 1964: Achtemeyer and Achtemeyer, 1962).

To understand how the Bible can help us translate Hebrew words, it is helpful to consider in context the conduct that characterizes the *resaim* in the Psalms in order to be able to identify an English word that might be used to translate *resaim*. They are people who are violent to the weak (e.g. Ps. 11: 5; 18: 48); exploit orphans (e.g. 10: 14-15; 82: 3-4); exploit widows (94: 3, 6; 146: 9); are bloodthirsty (51: 14; 55: 23); oppressors (63: 9; 73: 8); exploiters (35: 10); cunning (10: 7; 72: 14); tell lies (41: 8; 144: 8, 11); deceive people (28: 3; 40: 4); use fraud (5: 6; 109: 2); accept bribes (26: 10); do not repay (37: 21); are unmerciful (43: 1; 109: 16); and practice injustice (64: 6; 125: 3). We cannot spiritualize this data. The people are unjust. What they are doing is to benefit themselves financially at the expense of other people who they make poor. This is economic oppression: it is not primarily psychologically troubling someone because they believe in God (though it may include that), because oppressors also oppress people who are not believers. The Bible describes these oppressors according to their horizontal relationship with the neighbour, not according to their vertical relationship with God. We therefore cannot use the words 'wicked' or 'atheists'. 'Sinners' is equivocal, since the only sin mentioned is injustice. The appropriate way to translate *resaim* is, therefore, 'the unjust'. These are doers of *'awen* , that is, of iniquity. Ps. 1, 9 and 37 show that *resaim* and *saddikim*, a cognate of *sedeq*, are correlatives, therefore it is fair to translate *saddikim* as 'the just'. 'Unjust' appears 82 times in the Psalms: 'just' appears 52 times.

Judgment or justice?
Gaebelein (1980), who was style committee chairman for the NIV, identified that *mispat* means 'justice' on 91 of the 295 times it appears in the Old Testament, compared with its frequent translation as 'judgment' (Leclerc, 2001, Miranda, 1982).

Chapter 8
The Bible doctrine of justice - 2 New Testament

'North American evangelicals may journey to Korea to learn to pray and grow churches. They have yet to find their way to Atlanta to learn how to do justice' (Pannell, 1989).

'I cannot create a world apart from the realities of injustice. My every breath is a compromise with injustice.... A mirror held up to our world reflects the rupture of justice and the reign of injustice' (Lebacqz, 2007).

Here I consider Lee's argument that we should use the then contemporary Greek usage of *dikaiosune*, rather than relying on its use in the Septuagint to translate *sedeq*, as the basis on which to decide the meanings of *dikaiosune* in different contexts. I look at Crosby's and Tamez' comments on justice in the NT.

The unmarked (default or usual) meaning of *dikaiosune*

Dikaiosune is the Greek word that is used in the Septuagint version of the OT to translate *sedeq* (see chapter 7). Bosch (1991) indicates that in the NT *dikaiosune* could be translated justification (God's action of declaring us just), righteousness (either an attribute of God or a spiritual quality we receive from God) or justice (God's or our actions to right wrongs done to oppressed peoples).

Max Lee (2014) says that David Hill (1967) has made the point that when we read soteriological words such as the Greek word *dikaiosune* in the NT we should understand their meaning by going back via the use of *dikaiosune* in the Septuagint and substitute for *dikaiosune* the meaning of the Hebrew words *sedeq* and *sedaqa* that *dikaiosune* translated in the Septuagint. In my opinion there are at least two problems with this. First, the Septuagint was translated from the Hebrew Bible (OT) starting in 3rd century BCE although not finishing until the 2nd century CE. Between the 3rd century BCE and the 1st century CE when Paul is writing there might have been some changes in word usage in *koine* (common) Greek. Lee says that it is unrealistic to think that Paul might have expected his use of *dikaiosune* to be understood if he gave it a meaning that was not normally expected by 1st century CE Greek speakers. Secondly, as we saw in chapter 7, the main meaning of *sedeq/sedaqa* is contested, with, for example, perhaps the majority of English translations preferring 'righteousness' for most occurrences, while many language translations other than English prefer 'justice' as they translate it.

To clarify the unmarked meaning of *dikaiosune*, Lee extensively checks the development in the meaning of *dikaiosune* and its cognates from the time of Homer

(9th-11th century BCE) to 1st century CE in Greek secular literature, giving many examples and interpreting their meanings (see also Lee, 2015). Lee does not, however, claim to have completed a statistical analysis of word usage. Amongst his findings, the unmarked, default, primary meaning of *dikaios* (adjective) is its social use as 'right, fitting, appropriate and customary', although at times overlapping with its legal use as 'just, equitable, fair, lawful'. *Dikaios* occurs 80 times in the NT. The unmarked primary meaning of *dikaiosune* (noun) is 'justice' or distributive justice in its social and legal uses. *Dikaiosune* occurs 92 times in the NT. The unmarked, primary use of *dikaioo* (verb) is 'deem right, appropriate and fitting' or 'be in the right' according to society's expectations or laws governing community life. *Dikaioo* occurs 39 times in the NT. Lee also identifies the different marked (contextual or irregular) meanings that these cognates might have in certain contexts, based on examples in Greek literature over the period he researched, where the unmarked meaning might not best convey the meaning in that context.

Lee says that Biblical commentators run into problems when they blur the unmarked, default use of *dikaiosune* and its cognates with their specialized use in certain contexts. What some have tried to do is to look at quotes from the Old Testament that Paul uses, then reach back to *sedeq* via the Septuagint and then try to impose a specialized contextual reading from the Old Testament into the New Testament passage.

Lee compares the taxonomy of meanings for *dikaiosune* and its cognates with the lexical meanings given in Bauer (1979). Bauer is at its best when it classifies a meaning, usually where an OT text is quoted, as specialized in its context. However, since Lee also classifies this meaning as marked and specialized, Lee's classification agrees in this with Bauer. The problem arises, however, when Bauer labels a specialized Septuagintal usage as a major semantic classification. The problem with Bauer is that this lexicon is over dependent on Septuagintal usage when deciding on major semantic categories.

Finally, Lee tests in what ways commentators have identified specialized meanings of *dikaiosune* and its cognates that are different from their *koine* usage and what intertexts, such as OT or Jewish, inform these specialized meanings. He pilots this approach using Romans 3: 21-26, a well-known passage showing Paul's vocabulary on justification. In this passage there are four occurrences of *dikaiosune,* all four translated 'justice' in the Douay Rheims version, and one occurrence each of *dikaioumenoi, dikaion* and *dikaiounta*. Lee investigates the meanings claimed by a range of contemporary Biblical exegetes. He finds that all of these would fall within the range of meanings that he finds within 1st century *koine* Greek, so the taxonomy of meanings that he has constructed is robust. If a commentator's meaning falls outside Lee's taxonomy, the commentator would need to indicate what OT or Jewish intertexts might support their specialized meaning.

Crosby (1981) says that in prophesying the coming of Jesus, Jeremiah calls him, 'The Lord our justice' (Jer. 23: 6, New American Bible). In the same way as Jesus ministered God's justice, God wants us to minister God's justice, saying of his people, 'they shall be called in it the mighty ones of justice ... with the robe of justice he hath covered me ... so shall the Lord God make justice to spring forth, and praise before all the nations' (Is. 61: 3d, 10b, 11cd). Tracing *dikaiosune* through Matthew's gospel, we find Jesus in the Sermon on the Mount saying, 'Blessed are they that hunger and thirst after justice: for they shall have their fill' (Matt. 5: 6). In the wilderness of the Exodus, Israel had to learn to depend on God for the provision of their food and drink. Fasting helps us come to appreciate what it's like for the many in the world who go hungry daily, and to hear their cry for justice. Lowell Noble (2012) says Jesus was crucified because he identified with people on the margins of society, and because he didn't embrace the status quo but confronted a system that oppressed the poor. It is hardly surprising that Jesus also said, 'Blessed are they that suffer persecution for justice' sake: for theirs is the kingdom of heaven' (Matt. 5: 10), and, 'Seek ye therefore first the kingdom of God and his justice, and all these things shall be added unto you' (Matt. 6: 33).

One-third of all the NT occurrences of *dikaiosune* are in the book of Romans. We will look here primarily at how the need for justice helps us understand the calls from Majority World Christians for a more relevant understanding of the doctrine of justification by faith. Elsa Tamez (1993) says that justification by faith is popularly understood in Latin America as forgiveness of a sinner's sins, liberation from a person's guilt by Christ's blood shed on the cross and reconciliation with God through God's work alone. The main problem is that this formulation of the doctrine which they have received from the West makes it out of touch with most people's experience in Latin America.

Meanwhile the response of liberation theologians from Latin America indicating the need for oppressed people to engage politically to break free from their oppression has been characterized by some in the West as believing that God will save people by their works, rather than by their faith. However, people in Latin America are convinced they can only be saved by faith alone and that the political action is works that give evidence of their faith.

The reality for people from the Majority World is that while they are most aware that they are sinners, they are also the 'sinned-against', people who struggle under the oppression of structural sin. To explain structural sin, Gerald West (2005) explains the Temple system shown in Mark 11: 11-13: 2. Against a background of God's intention that the Jews should have equal plots of land, the priests and other political leaders, including the Roman occupiers, took advantage of God's requirements for people to give tithes and offerings to impose a system of exploitation and domination on the common people by which they became rich and powerful and the common people became poor and many were suffering exclusion from Temple worship (see chapter 5 above). Jesus' responses include overturning the tables and condemning the system as one of 'robbers'; encouraging a lone scribe who is interested in knowing who Jesus is; commending a poor woman for her offering; and condemning the Temple to be 'thrown down'.

West admits that apartheid in South Africa was a similar system of structural sin from which white people benefitted and that white people worldwide still continue to benefit from the neo-liberal capitalist system of globalization at the expense of the rest of the world. Not being aware of that system of structural sin, like the lone scribe (Mark 12: 28) and the rich man (Mark 10: 17) does not make people any the less a beneficiary of structural sin. In response West says Jesus makes it clear to the rich man in Mark 10: 21 that he needs to forsake the benefits of structural sin, return those benefits to the poor, and only at that point to follow Jesus. People then need to go on and dismantle the structural sin by changing the system.

The results of structural sin, which appear largely in the Majority World, are shown on the Global Issues website, and are listed in chapter 1 above.

For people in the West, a justification that relieves a person of guilt, without the need for a change in practice is a travesty of true justification. Similarly, for people from a Majority World background, an emphasis that justification all comes from the action of God, thereby implying the inferiority of people to God, should not prevent those people from seeing that they are children of God, as well as being encouraged to work for their liberation. To limit justification to the divine-human vertical relationship alone, while ignoring the inter-human horizontal justice implicit in *dikaiosune,* shows the weakness of the traditional view of justification.

In the West, Tom Wright (1992) has drawn people's attention to the fact that much Christian doctrine seems to have been formulated in an ahistorical way, without much connection at all between theology and history and that there is a need to reformulate these doctrines in such a way that we bring theology and history, and by implication context, together. Tamez says the current historical context in Latin America, caused by the imposition of neo-liberal globalization, is that for most people their basic material needs for food, work, shelter and education are hardly being met at all. A second issue is that people who have traditionally suffered discrimination – women, Black and indigenous peoples and Mestizos (people with mixtures of two cultures with opposite histories) – are still being trodden down and see themselves as non-persons. Justification that affirms life must have the face of the poor, addressing their economic oppression, including the sin of those oppressing them, and their human dignity.

Paul asked believers to present their bodies 'as instruments of justice unto God' (Rom. 6: 13). As a Jew from the diaspora, Paul recognized the discrimination that resulted in Jews having to pay more taxes than local citizens. But he also opposed Jewish exclusion of Gentiles from the kingdom of God. Working as an artisan as a tentmaker, Paul often had to work night and day (1 Thess. 2: 9) and knew what it was to have little as well as to have much (Phil. 4: 12). Paul was imprisoned in several places. People who were poor, slaves or foreigners got harsh punishment under the Romans, while the rich and privileged got away with lesser punishment.

While the book of Romans might be considered to be his central statement on the doctrine of justification by faith, Paul made a number of points on the subject in earlier letters, including 1 Thessalonians, 1 and 2 Corinthians, Galatians and Philippians. Paul speaks of the life and ministry of Jesus, not only of his death and resurrection. Justice and justification are the central theme of Galatians, arguing against Judaizers. There Paul contrasted the way that the works of the law enslave while faith enables liberation. Paul's chief focus was on the present life of Christians, in which people suffer and have every type of difficulty.

Christians in Rome mainly lived in a very poor part of the city. Many people from around the empire converged on Rome, particularly slaves, who would have been taken there as prisoners of war from rebellions in different provinces. Romans 1: 16-17 might be considered Paul's main theme: 'For I am not ashamed of the gospel. For it is the power of God unto salvation to everyone that believeth: to the Jew first and to the Greek. For the justice of God is revealed therein, from faith unto faith, as it is written: The just man liveth by faith'. God can transform oppressors and oppressed people into women and men who do justice to transform the unjust world.

Immediately after the statement in 1: 16-7, Paul reveals the wrath of God against people's impiety and injustice (*adikias*) in vv. 18 and 29. The first two chapters of Romans, explaining the sinful situation of society, are couched in terms of 'injustice', rather than the vaguer word 'sin'. By juxtaposing truth and injustice, Paul shows injustice as a lie and justice as the truth (c.f. 3: 5-7). In the Roman world, as today, the system presents itself as truth whereas the poor know it is injustice.

Summing up our motivation, Paul says, '(T)he kingdom of God is not meat and drink; but justice, and peace, and joy in the Holy Ghost' (Rom. 14: 17).

Chapter 9
Can the global rich get to heaven?

'At the least – I must face the blood on my own hands, on my face. It is not mere metaphor. The clothes I wear are scarlet under the infrared of spirit. They are not innocent of what has been shed around the world in their procurement at prices I like. The body I inhabit is burgundy white, full of dried blood of all whose dreams have been buried with them at the far end of my privilege and the gun I employ to ensure it. I eat others. I am born of their sweat and carved fat, their crushed life chances, their forced labour and raped vaginas and starved kids and untreated diseases and early deaths. My earthly destiny of delight depends upon theirs of damnation' (Perkinson, 2004).

Jesus speaks more about money than any other subject than the kingdom of God/heaven. Here I look at Matt. 25: 31-46 and ask how people will explain being complicit in oppressing the Majority World when Jesus says he will view how people have treated him by how they have treated the least of Jesus' brothers and sisters. Jesus is looking for people to change the system in the direction of justice, not for them to give a handout, which changes nothing. I end with practical suggestions from Majority World theologians.

In chapter 5 we looked briefly at the story of the rich man and Lazarus (Luke 16: 19-31). The story showed that the rich man had the wrong attitude towards earthly possessions in that he ignored Lazarus and treated his dogs better than his neighbour. Jesus says that there is sufficient information in the Old Testament ('Moses and the prophets') to guide rich people as to what to do so as to get to heaven, yet there is no evidence of repentance on the part of the rich man or his brothers. How should the global rich, including white Christians, understand Jesus' teaching with respect to themselves? How can they get to heaven? Is giving to charity enough? Is giving overseas aid to Majority World countries sufficient? Doesn't Christian Economics say that people need to operate according to the free market, so why should they want to redistribute earnings? Do people get to heaven by just believing the gospel and then God tests the rest of their works by fire? Isn't it that you should have the right attitude towards your money? Isn't it OK to keep your money providing you're willing for God to take it away from you (whether God does or doesn't take it away)?

In chapter 6 we saw how that Jesus in his statement of his vision (Luke 4: 18-19) was indicating that His kingdom was about bringing in the jubilee (Lev. 25) from its beginning by means of the rich giving their wealth to the poor and needy. Also in chapter 6, the analysis of Acts 1-12 showed that the early church took that sharing of their wealth with the poor as being a central part of their daily lifestyle in the Christian community. As such they were modeling this to the watching world.

Jesus speaks more about money than about prayer, in fact, more than about any other subject except the Kingdom of God/heaven. So money is clearly very important in his teaching. Somehow this subject creeps into what Miranda sees as the only detailed treatment of the Last Judgment in the Bible (Matt. 25: 31-46). He also identified the Last Judgment as being the point at which final justice is given to oppressed peoples and the unjust are punished. The righteous are accepted based on how they have responded to the needs of the least of Jesus' sons and daughters. This activity is mentioned four times, showing how important it is for us to take it to heart and act on it:

'For I was hungry and you gave me to eat;
I was thirsty, and you gave me to drink;
I was a stranger and you took me in:
naked, and you covered me:
sick, and you visited me:
I was in prison and you came to me'. (Matt. 25: 35-36; cf. vv. 38-39; 42-4).

Those who have done these things to the least of Jesus' sons and daughters worldwide are those who have done them to Jesus and therefore they are saved. Those who have not done this to the poorest of believers worldwide have not done it to Jesus and are therefore not saved. Those who see their salvation resulting from faith alone in Christ may see this parable as indicating people are justified by their works and they may react by seeing these things as add-ons to their faith. As we saw in chapters 5 and 6, however, the NT has a different way of testing whether people have faith in Christ, based on concrete horizontal love to the brother or neighbour, shown by practical works of mercy of the sort mentioned in Matt. 25, as opposed to a spiritualized vertical relationship based on what we say is faith alone.

'What shall it profit, my brethren, if a man say he hath faith, but hath not works? Shall faith be able to save him? And if a brother or sister be naked, and want daily food: and one of you say to them, "Go in peace, be ye warmed and filled", yet give them not those things that are necessary for the body, what shall it profit? So faith also, if it have not works, is dead in itself' (James 2: 14-17). For James, faith is only faith when it is accompanied by acts of jubilee towards the poor and oppressed. Otherwise, it is not faith.

'If any man say, "I love God", and hateth his brother; he is a liar. For he that loveth not his brother, whom he seeth, how can he love God, whom he seeth not' (1 John 4. 20). 'He that hath the substance of this world, and shall see his brother in need, but shall shut up his bowels from him: how doth the charity of God abide in him? My little children, let us not love in word, nor in tongue, but in deed, and in truth' (1 John 3: 17-18). John says that we show our love to our brothers and sisters when we live the jubilee in our actions towards the least of the oppressed.

This does not mainly mean the oppressed in our church but oppressed believers worldwide. If we are not living out the jubilee towards the least of believers worldwide we do not love God. Jesus, the Judge, of course, lived himself in increasing identification with poor and oppressed people during his life on earth

Robert McAfee Brown says that with respect to this passage Majority World believers challenge the global rich in three further ways. First, Jose Miranda reminded us in chapter 7 that the words translated 'righteous' and 'unrighteous' actually mean 'just' and 'unjust'. This is not a charitable handout that Jesus is asking people to give in a paternalistic way, showing that they are better than the poor. It is not the 'caring for the poor' that Western expositors encourage us to do (e.g. Green, 2000). 'Caring for the poor' keeps the exploitation the same as it ever was: the rich stay rich and the poor stay poor. This is a vote for keeping the status quo of exploitation and oppression. Rather it is restitution that the rich need to do: giving back to people what the rich have stolen from them that is rightfully theirs. This is the jubilee that Jesus said he was bringing to the world in his ministry.

Also, Gutierrez says we need to avoid thinking about this in terms of individual acts of charity with other individuals. There is the sad story of a person finding drowning babies in a stream every day. The person realized they needed to go upstream in order to find who was throwing the babies into the stream (ELCA, n.d.). Being a neighbour requires us to work not just with individuals. People need to start thinking about a 'collectivized charity: a whole system where injustice no longer exists' (Cardenal, 1982). Gutierrez's (1985) view is that this requires replacing the existing system by getting rid of 'the private ownership of the means of production' so that we can develop a system which benefits all of the people. This might need to take place step by step.

Finally, Gutierrez shows us that it is not individuals that are on trial, but 'all nations shall be gathered together before him, and he shall separate them one from another, as the shepherd separateth the sheep from the goats' (Matt. 25: 32). The nations are on trial. How does our own nation shape up?

Does our nation give drink to the thirsty and food to the hungry among the world's poorest people? Britain has been engaging in quiet negotiations for a number of years as part of the EU to change their terms of trade with 80 of the poorest countries in the Caribbean, Africa and the Pacific (APC countries) for the worse for those countries for the next 25 years, in so-called Economic Partnership Agreements (EPAs). The negotiating has been characterized as nothing short of blackmail. European farmers are already subsidized more per day for their cattle than the poor worldwide receive per day, showing that white people put a higher priority on their animals than on Africans, Asians and Latin Americans of humanity. British companies have been trying to get poor Ghanaians to pay for their water, while Shell has been the major contributor towards ruining the Niger Delta.

Does this nation of ours welcome strangers? In *CG* chapter 2 I have shown some increasingly oppressive ways in which Britain treats migrants. People who have come as asylum seekers from the Majority World are not wanted in UK to work under current policy for migrants. Asylum seekers are being sent back to all countries from which they have come regardless of what that country will do to them on their return.

Does this nation clothe the naked? Current policy is to make asylum seekers destitute through refusing them the opportunity to work for money and refusing failed asylum seekers state benefits. It is also state policy to force asylum seekers to give up their children into state care if they are found financially unable to care for them. Britain no longer aims to provide full employment: only around 70% of those aged 18-65 are today economically active.

Does this nation visit the sick? Why is it that Africa and India are suffering so much from AIDS when the West, which had the majority of HIV/AIDS sufferers worldwide in the late 1980s, has drugs that can save people's lives? Why is it today that 21,000 children under the age of five in the Majority World die every day from preventable diseases which they did not do before colonialism?

Does this nation visit people in prison? Why is it that there are more African-Caribbean young men in our prisons than go to university each year? Why is it that disproportionate numbers of African and Asian communities in Britain have had their DNA checked? Why are asylum seekers from the Majority World greeted in Britain with removal centres with conditions that are little different from prison (Border and Immigration Agency, 2007)?

Are there nations that are 'just' according to these criteria? One example is Cuba. In spite of the United States-inspired blockade, national programmes ensure there is enough shared around so people avoid going hungry or thirsty. Strangers are welcomed, wherever they come from. In order to clothe the naked employment for all is an aim while shelter is shared pending the building of new homes. Free infirmaries are available and Cuban doctors are famed. There are political prisoners, but treatment is better than in much of the Western Hemisphere. Other countries going on a similar road in Latin America include Venezuela, Bolivia and Argentina.

Barbara Ward said at a WCC conference: 'Christians alone straddle the whole spectrum of rich nations, and therefore Christians are a lobby or can be a lobby of incomprehensible importance.... And if we don't do it and we come ultimately before our Heavenly Father, and he says, "Did you feed them, and did you give them to drink, did you clothe them, did you shelter them"? and we say, "Sorry, Lord, but we did give them 0.3% of our gross national product," I don't think it will be enough' (World Conference on Church and Society, 1967). Particularly not in view of the net flows of money from poor to rich countries since 1970 noted in *CG* chapter 3.

Rene Kruger (2004) has useful comments on Jesus' ministry in Luke's gospel. Speaking as he does from Buenos Aires he reads the Bible from a 'context of poverty, exclusion, violence, corruption and destruction of life'. He comments on Jesus' sermon on the plain, in the light of the fact that of 235 occurrences (Hebrew *rash*, *'ebyon*, *dal*, *'ani*) of the word 'poor' in the Old Testament, 210 refer to the materially poor and just 25 *('anaw)* refer to spiritually poor, while in the New Testament all except one of the occurrences of the word 'poor' (*ptochos*) refer to the materially poor. This has a different feel from Matthew's Beatitudes:

'And he, lifting up his eyes on his disciples, (Jesus) said,

"Blessed are ye poor,

for yours is the kingdom of God.

Blessed are ye that hunger now:

for you shall be filled.

Blessed are ye that weep now:

for you shall laugh.

Blessed shall you be when men shall hate you,

and when they shall separate you, and shall reproach you,

and cast out your name as evil, for the Son of Man's sake.

Be glad in that day and rejoice;

For behold, your reward is great in heaven.

For according to these things did their fathers to the prophets.

But woe to you that are rich:

for you have your consolation.

Woe to you that are filled:

for you shall hunger.

Woe to you that now laugh:

for you shall mourn and weep.

Woe to you when men shall bless you:

for according to these things did their fathers to the false prophets"'. (Luke 6: 20-26).

Kruger says, 'By setting the two groups in a parallel opposition, Luke declares that the poor are poor because the rich *have made them* poor; the hungry are hungry because those who are satisfied *have made them* hungry; those who cry do so because those who laugh make them cry; and the persecuted *suffer* because the prestigious, flattered, and famous *persecute* them' (italics his).

I found it very helpful to pray through each statement in this passage comparing in parallel each blessing of the poor and woe of the rich. This is the world that Majority World Christians speak of, according to Gutierrez: oppressors and the oppressed, the rich and the poor. Jesus has identified himself with the poor. Kruger notes the conflict running throughout Luke between the rich and the poor: the two are opposed in each case. There are no independent poor and no independent, innocent rich.

In a traditional white explanation of this passage, Michael Wilcock (1979) says first that Luke 6: 20-49 is Luke's counterpart to Matthew's version of the Sermon on the Mount in Matthew 5, 6 and 7. He acknowledges that Luke misses out Jesus' fulfillment of Old Testament law in Matt. 5: 17-48. The reason Wilcock gives for this is that in Luke, Jesus is giving out a new form of law to replace the old law. He then identifies the people who are blessed as 'God's people', who have different values from the world. In spite of what has been said, unambiguously, about the materially poor and rich, throughout the Bible, especially in the Psalms, he allows the one occurrence of 'poor in spirit' in Matt. 5: 3 to justifying his spiritualization of Luke's poor and rich to mean 'believers' and 'the world'.

Gutierrez (1985) is helpful on these two passages. He sees poverty as a scandalous condition that degrades human beings and needs to be done away with, since it is also against God's will. Gutierrez says 'spiritual poverty' was a phrase used since the seventh century BCE, by prophets such as Zephaniah and Isaiah, to refer to the remnant that God would bring back from exile (e.g. Zeph. 3: 12-13; Is. 6: 13). This 'poor' person was open to God or humble before God. This is therefore a spiritual childhood. So Matt. 5: 3 refers to people who are totally at God's disposal, to do God's will, as Christ was. This, however, cannot be used as a justification for hanging on to hoarded resources (Luke 12: 13-21), as often happens in the West. Luke 6: 20-26, in contrast to Matt. 5: 3, refers to the materially poor. But it does not say, 'accept your poverty, because you will be rich in the next life'. When we looked at Luke 4: 18-19 in ch. 6 we saw that this indicated that the Kingdom of God that Jesus brought meant jubilee now, that is, justice in this life, something that all the OT prophets believed in as well. Therefore, the poor are blessed as a result of the fact that the Kingdom of God has begun, because they are now going to get justice from global rich believers in this life. So, firstly, it is the responsibility of the church today to do what the New Testament church did towards poor Christians in the worldwide church (c.f. Rom. 15: 26), not just to poor Christians in their own church:

'And all they that believed, were together, and had all things common. Their possessions and goods they sold, and divided them to all, according as every one had need'. (Acts 2: 44-45). 'The multitude of believers had but one heart and one soul: neither did any one say that aught of the things which he possessed, was his own; but all things were common unto them.... (N)either was there any one needy among them. For as many as were owners of land or houses, sold them, and brought the price of the things they sold, and laid it down before the feet of the apostles. And distribution was made to every one, according as he had need'. (Acts 4: 32, 34, 35).

This is not setting up poverty as an ideal: rather it is making sure that there are no longer any poor people. But also the poor person is fighting for liberation from their oppressors. So, secondly, we also need to come alongside poor people as a materially poor church and materially poor Christians, so that we can then work with the poor so that they gain liberation from their oppressors by our showing that we are spiritually poor, that is open to the future that God has promised of justice in the Kingdom of God in this life.

The encounter with the rich young ruler (Luke 18: 18-30) indicates the stumbling block of the young man's unwillingness to give his money to the poor and follow Jesus. This giving up of riches to the poor was done in the case of Jesus (who increasingly identified with the poor), the disciples ('we left all we had'), Zacchaeus (Luke 19) and the early church in Jerusalem. It follows the poverty of the Levites, who had no inheritance, and of the Old Testament prophets. Commenting on the story of the rich young ruler, Kosuke Koyama (1980-1) says that Jesus' life was a journey from the centre of life to the periphery that ended at the cross.

For Kruger, Luke has three themes in his economic and social analysis: the massive gap between poor and rich, Jesus' judgment on the rich and solidarity with the poor, and how people do sharing. The poor's situation is not a virtue but they do have the solidarity of God. The poor lack basic material needs for life, know sorrow, hunger and persecution. The Beatitude above encourages overthrowing poverty. Jesus (for example, in Luke) and the early church (Acts. 1-12) engaged in a series of liberatory actions, through healing and resurrection. These enabled people to be restored in their human dignity, in health, to be able to work and know God. This inverts society from one worshipping success and power to one uplifting the poor.

Jesus' challenge to the global rich is to give their wealth to the poor and to follow him. Following Jesus' criticism of the rich, this is the opportunity of conversion for the rich. Zacchaeus gives half of his wealth to the poor (Luke 19: 1-10). Why can't white Christians do the same? It is because white Christians will not do this that they have to resort to spiritualization of what Jesus says about money and the rich, trying to say that it's one's 'inner attitude' that counts. Why is it that they insist that other people should not spiritualize the Bible, yet it is alright for them to spiritualize Jesus' teaching on money, the rich and the poor, or to think that it's only celebrities who are the rich? Jesus says that Mammon is money unjustly gained (Luke 16: 9 *adikias*). In Luke, he shows a number of ways in which this Mammon can be shared, for example, through selfless giving (7: 36-50), putting yourself at the disposal of others (8: 1-3); giving without expecting return (6: 34-35); and lowering debts (16: 5-7).

Somehow I cannot understand 6: 20-26 unless it is in terms of renouncing riches and working with the global poor towards their liberation. This means not only giving your money to the global poor but also struggling with them towards their liberation. All people need to work together for justice and liberation because God is working in the world for liberation of the oppressed (Kairos Document, 1986).

Some might say that non-Christians can give their money to the poor. What shows that you're Christian when you do this? Acts 10: 38 says of Jesus' ministry, 'God anointed him with the Holy Ghost, and with power, who went about doing good, and healing all that were oppressed by the devil, for God was with him.' There's not just the 'doing good' but also the 'healing all that were oppressed by the devil'. Display of the gifts of the Spirit (c.f. Matt. 10: 7-8) is something only Christians can do.

To give a taster of how Majority World Christians feel about the pain of being poor and how they want white Christians to struggle alongside them for a more just world I summarise here a paper by Asian Christian theologians from a conference in Sri Lanka.

'Thou shalt not worship other gods: towards a decolonizing theology' (EATWOT, 2002).

In a refugee camp we met Muslims who have been forced to leave their homes by the Tamil Tigers. The Muslims had been seen as undesired criminals. In another refugee camp we met Tamil people crowded into a large hall. Conflict has resulted from British colonial rule and ethnic confrontation since independence. This theological reflection is in the context of three predominant realities in Asia: first, continued colonial domination over people, resources and land; then, manipulation of religions for the legitimacy of the ruling class; finally, exploitation of people based on caste, language group, ethnicity and gender.

Two major changes have happened under globalization. First, the market has become the main agency for social and individual mediation. Religious practices, health care and education are now brought within the neo-liberal ideology of the market. The market becomes the true 'ecclesia' or church. Success in the market results from being able to transform everything into commodities, so people become labour or prostitutes, land becomes golf parks or raw materials, while culture becomes souvenirs. All is done for self-interest. Those who have no commodities are excluded from the market. It is estimated that 20% of the population will keep the world economy going, so 80% of the population is expendable and is unwanted.

Second, as money has become the storehouse of value, 'having' determines 'being'. As finance capital flies round the world, money market dealers act in the global casino, skimming the surplus from peasants and workers worldwide. A 'United States of Owners of Capital' comprising Japan, Western Europe and North America, together with the Asian Tigers, rules the world. While women's bodies become commodities, they are also the largest group of consumers. The market thereby creates a crisis in women and turns people into puppets in the market-place.

We need to develop theological reflection prior to new action. First, to consider how to deal with colonialism in all its manifestations, re-ordering land and the international division of labour, restoring resources to the colonized, reordering market domination, restoring people's cultures, replacing market domination with the people's governance and shifting economic considerations from expanding value to sustaining life. Then, liberation of religion and faith from the captivity of the market and politics. Also, to rid the world of exploitation of women. Further, to identify effective dialogue between different ethnic groups and faiths. The proposals are as follows.

First, we need to be with the God of life against the ungod of death. Being with God means seeing and hearing the people's oppression and cry and engaging with their lives for their liberation (see Exod. 3: 7-9). We need to denounce the market, which has divinized money, that is, money-theism. The Church and Christian faith has sold out to the market in its role since 1492. Money-theism has loosened the sovereignty of the nation state resulting in marginalization of the poor and undermining of culture. We need different ethnic groups to reclaim their cultures from the homogenous market culture, yet critiquing cultures using Gal. 3:28, cultures need to affirm the rights of the weak. There needs to be eco-justice and gender-justice as well as human rights. Since the church is global it needs to build global solidarity against the global power of the market.

Then, the spirituality of resistance. The jubilee was instituted as a development of observing the Sabbath. The jubilee ensures participation of nature together with people in God's holiness. This is through equality. 'The seventh is the day of the Sabbath, that is, the rest of the Lord thy God. Thou shalt not do any work therein, thou, nor thy son nor thy daughter, nor thy manservant nor thy maidservant, nor thy ox, nor thy ass, nor any of thy beasts, nor the stranger that is within thy gates: that thy manservant and thy maidservant may rest, even as thyself' (Deut. 5: 14). The jubilee and Sabbath year demand institutional assurance of justice and equality and holistic relationship with nature and people. Aspects include first, rest and Sabbath for nature and people; then, redistributing wealth, resources and land to ensure equality; also, canceling debt; further, liberating slaves. Sabbath and jubilee counter globalization and growth. This includes debt forgiveness and also restitution of what has been stolen back to the place it belongs. This is how people can become properly related to God. Reconciliation depends on restitution, ending global apartheid (Is. 65: 20-25).

Also, the land is God's (Lev. 25: 23, Ps. 8), not man's. Western thought has objectified nature and made the earth a commodity for plundering. God, community and land are an axis that does not include exploitation and private property. The earth's exploitation reflects people's alienation from God. Colonisation resulted in white people grabbing land and others becoming landless. Land must be restored equitably. Holding resources and land without sharing them with the poor is a sin against other people and against God.

Further, re-discovering God's female face. C. McGhee Livers (2003) and Drorah O'Donnell Setel (1992) say that the name for God often in Genesis – *El-Shaddai* – means breast, indicating God's intention that people should multiply. People need to reorient from a patriarchal, domineering God to a Creator who both provides and nourishes life. Women need to take their rightful place in family, society and the church. Mary in her Magnificat shows this inverting of traditional power structures.

Finally, dialogue with other faiths requires respecting them, their value and dignity. There are a lot of practical principles that need to be learnt from other faiths. Cosmic harmony, equality as a principle for peace, compassion in the human divine relationship and overcoming suffering through controlling your desires are all lessons to be learned. We need to work together to forge communities of hope and resistance.

BIBLIOGRAPHY

Achtemeyer, Elizabeth R. (1962) Righteousness in the Old Testament, and Paul J. Achtemeyer, Righteousness in the New Testament, in *Interpreter's Dictionary of the Bible*, vol. R-Z, pp. 80-5, 91-9.

Adewale, Olubiyi Adeniyi. (2006). An Afro-sociological application of the parable of the rich man and Lazarus (Luke 16: 19-31), in *Black Theology: An International Journal, Vol. 4.1,* pp. 27-43. London: Equinox.

Alexander, Michelle. (2012). *The New Jim Crow*. New York: The New Press.

Alkalimat, Abdul Halimu Ibn. (1998). The ideology of Black social science. In Ladner, Joyce ed., *The death of white sociology* (pp. 173-189). Baltimore: Black Classic Pr.

Allen, Roland. (1979). *Missionary methods – St. Paul's or ours?* (pp. 135-150). Grand Rapids: Eerdmans.

Allen, Roland. (1978). *The spontaneous expansion of the Church and the causes which hinder it.* Grand Rapids: Eerdmans.

Amos, Clare. (2004). *The book of Genesis* (pp. 27-44, 226-9). Peterborough: Epworth.

Andrew, Revd. Hewlette (Hewie). (1990). Developing Black Ministries, in *Account of hope: report of a conference on the economic empowerment of the Black community* (p. 39). London: British Council of Churches.

Balasundaram, Franklyn J. (2001). William Carey, in Scott W. Sunquist, David Wu Chu Sing, John Chew Hiang Chea eds., *A dictionary of Asian Christianity* (pp. 119-121). Cambridge: Eerdmans.

Balia, Daryl. (2007). "True lies": American missionary sayings in South Africa (1835-1910) in *Black Theology: An International Journal* 5, no. 2, pp. 203-219.

Bauer, Walter. (1979). *A Greek-English Lexicon of the New Testament and other early Christian literature.* Second edition. Editors, W. F. Arndt, F. W. Gingrich and Frederick W. Danker. Chicago: University of Chicago Press.

Barrett, David B. and Todd M. Johnson. (2001/2). Definitions from World Christian encyclopaedia and World Christian trends in *International Bulletin of Missionary Research*, Vol 31, No 1, January 2007.

Barrett, David B. and Todd M. Johnson. (2003). *World Christian Trends*. Pasadena: William Carey Library.

Bebbington, David W. (1989). *Evangelicalism in modern Britain* (pp. 2-17). London: Unwin Hyman.

Beckford, Robert. (2000). *Dread and pentecostal* (pp. 8-18). London: SPCK.

Beckford, Robert. (1998). *Jesus is Dread*. London: Darton, Longman and Todd.

Bediako, Kwame. (1983). Biblical Christologies in the context of African traditional religions, in Vinay Samuel and Chris Sugden eds., *Sharing Jesus in the Two Thirds World* (pp. 117-135). Bangalore: Partnership in Mission-Asia.

Bediako, Kwame. (2005). Christian witness in the public sphere: some lessons and residual challenges from the recent political history of Ghana, in Lamin Sanneh & Joel A. Carpenter eds., *The changing face of Christianity* (p. 121). New York: OUP.

Bediako, Kwame. (2004). *Jesus and the gospel in Africa* (pp. 6, 85-96). Maryknoll: Orbis.

Bediako, Kwame. (1999). *Theology and identity* (pp. 174-222, 185, 433). Oxford: Regnum.

Behm, J.and E. Wurthwein, *noeo*, in Kittel's *Theological Dictionary of the New Testament*, vol. 4.

Bhavnani, Reena, Heidi Safia Mirza and Veena Meetoo. (2005). *Tackling the roots of racism* (pp. 55-8). Bristol: Policy Press.

Black Catholics, Congress of. (1990). London: Catholic Assoc. for Racial Justice.

Black Manifesto. (2010). *The price of race inequality*. http://cers.leeds.ac.uk/files/2013/05/Price-of-inequality-the-black-manifesto-2010.pdf

Bonk, Jonathan J. (1996). *Missions and money* (pp. 14-5, 85-107). New York: Orbis.

Border and Immigration Agency. (2007). Complaints Audit Committee, Annual Report for 2006/7
http://www.ind.homeoffice.gov.uk/6353/aboutus/cacreport0607.pdf

Bosch, David J. (1991). *Transforming mission* (p. 72). Maryknoll: Orbis.

Botterweck, G. Johannes. (1951). *"Gott Erkennen" im Sprachgebrauch des Alten Testaments* (p. 44). Bonn: Peter Hanstein.

Brierley, Peter. (2013). *Capital growth* (Table 3.7, p.64). Tonbridge: ADBC.

Brierley, Peter. (2014). *UK Church statistics number 2: 2010 to 2020*. Tonbridge: ADBC.

Brock, Peggy. (2005). *New Christians as evangelists*, in Norman Etherington ed., *Missions and empire*. Oxford: OUP.

Brown, Francis, S.R. Driver and Charles A. Briggs. (1991). *A Hebrew and English lexicon of the Old Testament*. Peabody: Hendrickson.

Brown, Robert McAfee. (1984). *Unexpected news*. Philadelphia: Westminster Press.

Burnard, Trevor. (2004). *Mastery, tyranny and desire: Thomas Thistlewood and his slaves in the Anglo-Jamaican world*. Chapel Hill: University of North Carolina Press.

Bush, Barbara. (1990). *Slave women in Caribbean society 1650-1838*. (p. 120). London: James Currey.

Buxton, C. ed. (1848). *Memoirs of Sir Thomas Fowell Buxton* (p. 360). London.

Calvin, John. (1986). Commentary on Habakkuk 2: 6. In *Commentary on Habakkuk, Zephaniah and Haggai.* Edinburgh: Banner of Truth.

Cardenal, Ernesto. (1982). *The gospel in Solentiname* (Vol. 4/ 51). Maryknoll: Orbis.

Carey, Lord George. (2006). *A communion in crisis?* Reflection at Virginia Theological Seminary, May 9th at
http://glcarey.co.uk/Speeches/2006/Communion%20in%20crisis.html

Carey, William. (1792). *An inquiry into the obligations of Christians to use means for the conversion of the heathen* (pp. 13, 63, 65). Leicester.

Chakrabortty, Aditya. (2015). The families being cheated out of their homes – for the sin of being poor. *The Guardian*, 13th January.

Choi, Yong-Joon. (2006). *Dialogue and antithesis: a philosophical study on the significance of Herman Dooyeweerd's transcendental critique.* Philadelphia: Hermit Kingdom.

Cone, James H. (2013). *The cross and the lynching tree.* Maryknoll: Orbis.

Collins, Patricia Hill. (2000). *Black feminist thought.* New York: Routledge.

Cooke, Sam. (1964). *A change is gonna come.* RCA.

Cooper, Michael T. (2003). *What is, and who defines, Evangelical Christianity?* at
http://www.opensourcetheology.net/node/72

Cooper, Michael T. (2005). Colonialism, neo-Colonialism and forgotten missiological lessons, *Global Missiology*, January.

Costas, Orlando. (1989). *Christ outside the gate* (pp. 29, n. 7,8,10 pp.39-42). Maryknoll: Orbis.

Costas, Orlando. (1983). Proclaiming Christ in the Two Thirds World, in Vinay Samuel and Chris Sugden eds., *Sharing Jesus in the Two Thirds World* (pp. 6-7). Bangalore: Partnership in Mission-Asia.

Costas, Orlando. (1973). Mission out of affluence. In *Missiology: An International Review*, 1(4), pp. 405-423.

Cress Welsing, Frances. (2010). *Surviving racism in the 21st century, part 1.*
https://www.youtube.com/watch?v=Zdblpa0AfuQ

Crosby, Michael. (1981). *Spirituality of the Beatitudes: Matthew's challenge for First World Christians* (pp. 118-39; 199-217). Maryknoll: Orbis.

Cross Jr., William E. (1991). *Shades of Black: diversity in African-American identity.* Philadelphia: Temple University Press.

DeGruy Leary, Joy A. (2005). *Post traumatic slave syndrome: America's legacy of enduring injury and healing.* (pp. 10-1). Milwaukie, Oregon: Uptone.

DeGruy, Joy Angela. (2009). *Post traumatic slave syndrome: America's legacy of enduring injury and healing. The study guide.* Portland: Joy DeGruy Publishing, Inc.

Derrida, Jacques. (1976). *Of Grammatology*, trans. Gayatri Chakravorty Spivak (pp. 158-9). Baltimore: Johns Hopkins University Press.

Dharampal. (1999). *Despoliation and defaming of India*, Vol. 1, p. 103. Goa: Other India Press.

Dharmaraj, Jacob S. (1993). *Colonialism and Christian mission* (p. 81). Delhi: ISPCK.

Doane, Ashley W. (2003). Rethinking whiteness studies. In Doane, Ashley W. and Eduardo Bonilla-Silva eds., *White Out: The Continuing Significance of Racism* (pp. 12-14). London: Routledge.

Donovan, Vincent J. (2006). *Christianity rediscovered* (pp. 3-14). London: SCM.

Dooyeweerd, Herman, D. F. M. Strauss (ed.), John Kraay (trans.). (2003). *The roots of Western culture*. Lewiston: Edwin Mellen.

Dooyeweerd, Herman. (1980). *In the twilight of Western thought: studies in the pretended autonomy of philosophical thought* (pp. 38-41). Nutley: Craig Press.

Douglass, Frederick. (1955). *Narrative of the life of Frederick Douglass, an American slave.* (pp. 105, 113). Mineola: Dover.

Draper, Nick et al. (2014). *Legacies of British slave-ownership*. Cambridge: CUP.

Du Bois, W. E. B. (1989). *The Souls of Black Folk* (p. 8). New York: Bantam.

Duchrow, Ulrich and Franz J. Hinkelammert. (2004). *Property for people, not for profit*. London: Zed Books/CIIR.

Durkheim, Emile. (1967). *De la división del trabajo social* (pp. 145-6). Steven M. Voth's translation. Buenos Aires: Schapire.

Dussel, Enrique. (1972). Hipotesis para una historia de la teologia en America Latina, in *Christus* (Mexico) 479, 1975, p. 9, in Enrique Dussel, *Historia de la Iglesia en America Latina* (Vol 2, pp. 306-42). Barcelona: Editorial Nova Terra.

EATWOT. (2002). Thou shalt not worship other gods: towards a de-colonizing theology, in Chung, Sook Ja and Marlene Perera eds., *Sustaining spiritualities with living faiths in Asia in the context of globalization* (pp. 131-48). Colombo: Centre for Society and Religion.

ELCA (Evangelical Lutheran Church of America) (n.d.) http://www.uss-elca.org/more-resources-for-advocacy-ministry

Elliott, Larry. (2005). Subsidising cows while milking the poor: the West should pay more attention to world poverty than protecting its farmers, in *The Guardian*, Monday October 17th.

Equality and Human Rights Commission. (2011). *How fair is Britain? Equality, human rights and good relations in 2010: first triennial review*. Manchester: EHRC.

Fields, B., K. Reesman, C. Robinson, A. Sims, K. Edwards, B. McCall, B. Short and S.P Thomas. (1998). Anger of African American women in the South (pp. 353-73). *Issues in mental health nursing, 19.*

Firth, Cyril B. (1961). *An introduction to Indian church history* (p. 137). Madras: The Christian Literature Society.

Fletchman Smith, Barbara. (2003). *Mental slavery: psychoanalytic studies of Caribbean people.* (pp. 23, 76). London: Karnac.

Fletchman Smith, Barbara. (2011). *Transcending the legacies of slavery: a psychoanalytic view*. (pp. 15-43). London: Karnac.

Fredrickson, George M. (1995). *Black liberation: a comparative history of Black ideologies in the United States and South Africa* (pp. 64, 65 n. 15). New York, OUP.

Freud, Sigmund. (1900). *The interpretation of dreams*. Standard Edition. Vols. IV-V. London: Hogarth Press.

Fung, Raymond. (1980). Good news to the poor – a case for a missionary movement, in *Your kingdom come: mission perspectives* (pp. 83-92). Geneva: WCC.

Gaebelein, Frank. (1980). Old Testament foundations for living more simply, in Ron Sider ed., *Living more simply*. London: Hodder and Stoughton.

Gaffin Jr., Richard B. (1996). A cessationist view, in Wayne Grudem ed., *Are miraculous gifts for today? Four views*. (pp. 26-64). Leicester: IVP.

Gairdner, W. H. T. (1910). *Edinburgh 1910, an account and interpretation of the World Missionary Conference* (pp. 141, 193). London: Oliphant, Anderson + Ferrier.

Gates Jr., Henry Louis. (2014). http://www.theroot.com/articles/history/2012/10/how_many_slaves_came_to_america_fact_vs_fiction.html

Gilroy, Paul. (2004). *After empire* (pp. 95-132). Abingdon: Routledge.

Global Issues website. http://www.globalissues.org/article/26/poverty-facts-and-stats

Gonzalez, Justo L. (1990). *Manana: Christian theology from a Hispanic perspective* (pp. 57-66). Nashville: Abingdon.

Gonzalez, Justo L. (2002). *Faith and wealth* (pp. 36-51). Eugene: Wipf and Stock.

Green, J. B. (1997). *The gospel of Jesus* (p. 608). Grand Rapids: Eerdmans.

Green, Michael. (2000). *The message of Matthew* (pp. 109, 262-5). Leicester: IVP.

Guha, Ranajit. (1992). Dominance without hegemony and its historiography, in Ranajit Guha ed., *Subaltern Studies VI* (pp. 210-309). Delhi: Oxford UP.

Gutierrez, Gustavo. (1985). *A theology of liberation*, trans. Sister Caridad Inda and John Eagleson eds. (pp. 202, 287-306). London: SCM.

Haenchen, Ernst. (1963). Der Vater, der mich gesandt hat, in *New Testament Studies* 9, no. 3, April, pp. 36-53.

Haley, Alex. (1991). *Roots* (p. 293). London: Vintage.

Hanks, Thomas D. (1984). *God so loved the Third World: the Biblical vocabulary of oppression*, trans. James C. Dekker (p. 40). Maryknoll: Orbis.

Hanson, K.C. and Douglas E. Oakman. (1998). *Palestine in the time of Jesus* (pp. 113-5). Minneapolis: Fortress.

Harling, Mack. (2005). De-Westernizing doctrine and developing appropriate theology in mission, *International Journal Frontier Missions*, 22:4, Winter, pp.159-66.

Harris-Perry, Melissa V. (2011). *Sister Citizen: shame, stereotypes and Black women in America.* New Haven: Yale UP.

Hart, Richard. (1998). *From occupation to independence: a short history of the peoples of the English-speaking Caribbean region.* (pp. 20-4). London: Pluto Press.

Hastings, Adrian. (1967). *Church and mission in modern Africa.* (p. 60). London: Burns and Oates.

Hawken, Paul. (2007). *Blessed unrest.* London: Penguin.

Heath, Roy. (1984). *The murderer.* London: Fontana.

Helms, Janet E. ed. (1990). *Black and white racial identity.* Westport: Greenwood.

Herzberg, Hans Wilhelm. (1922). Die Entwicklung des Begriffes mishpat im AT, in *Zeitschrift fur alttestamentliche Wissenschaft* 40, pp. 256-87.

Herzberg, Hans Wilhelm. (1923). Prophet und Gott, in *Beitrage zur Forderung der christlichen Theologie*, 28/3, pp. 23-4.

Hickford, Andy. (1998). *Essential youth.* (pp. 31-6). London: Kingsway.

Hill, David. (1967). *Greek words and Hebrew meanings: studies in the semantics of soteriological terms* (pp. 294-6). SNTSMS 5. Cambridge: CUP.

Hinkelammert, Franz J. (2006). The economic roots of idolatry, in Richard, Pablo et al., *The idols of death and the God of life* (pp. 165-93). Trans. Barbara E. Campbell and Bonnie Shepard. Eugene: Wipf and Stock.

Hinkelammert, Franz J. (1986). *The ideological weapons of death: a theological critique of Capitalism*, trans. Phillip Berryman. Maryknoll: Orbis.

Hofstadter, Richard. (1962). *Anti-intellectualism in American life.* New York: Vintage.

Holladay, William L, ed. (1971). *A concise Hebrew and Aramaic lexicon of the Old Testament.* Grand Rapids: Eerdmans.

Holsclaw, Geoff. (2004). *What African theologians can teach the Emerging Church* at http://www.emergingchurch.info .

Howard, Kweku. (1989). First West African prophet, in *West Africa*, no. 3776, pp. 2149-2151 (25th December 1989-7th January 1990).

Howell, Richard. (2001). The Hindu missionary movements and Christian missions in India, in W. Taylor ed., *Global missiology for the 21st century, The Iguassu dialogue* (p. 409). WEF.

Hurston, Zora Neale. (1937). *Their eyes were watching God* (p. 14). Philadelphia: J. B. Lippincott.

Isasi-Diaz, Ada Maria. (2000) Justice in Fabella, Virginia and R. S. Sugirtharajah eds., *Dictionary of Third World Theologies* (pp. 115-6). Maryknoll: Orbis.

Jackson, Samuel L. (2011). In David A. Keeps, Tell it on the mountain, Fall preview '11. *New York Times magazine*, August 21st.

James, George. (1976). *Stolen Legacy.* San Francisco: Julian Richardson Assocs.

Jasper, Lee. (2013). *What happens when a dream is deferred? 50 years on from Dr Martin Luther King's famous speech Lee Jasper Co Chair of BARAC asks; "Equality? Are we there yet?"*
http://blackactivistsrisingagainstcuts.blogspot.co.uk/2013/02/what-happens-when-dream-is-deferred-50.html

Jenkins, Paul. (1973). A forgotten vernacular periodical, *Mitteilungen der Basler Afrika Bibliographien*, vol 9, December, p. 29.

Jenkins, Philip. (2007). Lead speaker at *Global schism: Is the Anglican communion rift the first stage in a wider Christian split?*
http://pewforum.org/events/?EventID=145

Jeremias, Joachim. (1954). *The parables of Jesus* (p. 184). New York: Scribner.

Johnstone, Patrick. (1998). *The church is bigger than you think.* (pp. 89-90, 100, 114-5). Ross-shire/Gerrards Cross: Christian Focus/WEC.

Jones, Dana. (1987). The road to Celia's, *Evangelical Beacon*, 60, 16, August 31st.

Jones, P. R. (1982). *The teachings of the parables.* Nashville: Broadman.

Kairos Document, The. (1986). South African authors. Second edition (pp. 17-31).

Kidron, Michael & Ronald Segal. (1981). *The state of the world atlas* (Map 21. Dependence and diversity). London: Pan Books.

Karenga, Maulana. (1993). *Introduction to Black studies* (pp. 115-34, 220-3). Los Angeles: University Sankore Press.

King Jr., Dr. Martin Luther. (1967). Massey Lecture # 5. December 24th.

King M., E. Coker, G. Leavey, A. Hoare and E. Johnson-Sabine. (1994). Incidence of psychotic illness in London: comparison of ethnic groups. *British Medical Journal*, 309 (Oct 29): 1115-9.

Kings, Graham. (2003). *Canal, river and rapids: contemporary evangelicalism in the Church of England*, in *Anvil*, Vol. 20, No 3, September, pp. 167-184.

Kivel, Paul. (2011). *Uprooting racism: how white people can work for racial justice.* Gabriola Island: New Society publishers.

Koehler, Ludwig and Walter Baumgartner. (1958). *Lexicon in Veteris Testamenti Libros.* Leiden: Brill.

Koyama, Kosuke. (1980-1). Hallowed be your name, *International Review of Mission* 49, pp. 280-282.

Kraus, Hans-Joachim. (1957). *Die prophetische Verkundigung des Rechts in Israel* (p. 29). Zollikon: Evangelischer Verlag.

Kraybill, Donald B. (2003). *The upside-down kingdom* (pp. 72-83). Scottdale: Herald.

Kruger, Rene. (2004). Luke's God and mammon, A Latin American perspective, in *Global Bible Commentary*, eds. Daniel Patte, J. Severino Croatto, Nicole Wilkinson Duran, Teresa Okure and Archie Chi Chung Lee (pp. 395-400). Nashville: Abingdon.

Kwaku, ed. (2014). *Look how far we've come: The race/racism primer*. London: African Histories Revisited.

Lansley, Stewart and Joanna Mack. (2015). *Breadline Britain* (pp. 19-20). London: Oneworld.

Lebacqz, Karen. (2007). *Justice in an unjust world* (pp. 10-1). Minneapolis: Fortress.

Leclerc, Thomas. (2001). *Yahweh is exalted in justice: solidarity and conflict in Isaiah*. Minneapolis: Fortress.

Lee, Max J. (2014). Greek words and Roman meanings: Parts 1 and 2 – Remapping righteousness language. In Choi, Soon Bong, Jin Ki Hwang and Max J. Lee eds., *Fire in my soul: essays on Pauline soteriology and the gospels in honor of Seyoon Kim* (pp. 1-52). Eugene: Wipf and Stock.

Lee, Max J. (2015). *Moral transformation in Greco-Roman philosophy of mind: mapping the moral milieu of the apostle Paul and his diaspora Jewish contemporaries*. Tubingen: Mohr Siebeck.

Ligo, Arche. (2000). Oppression, in Fabella, Virginia and R. S. Sugirtharajah eds., *Dictionary of Third World Theologies* (p. 154). Maryknoll: Orbis.

Lorde, Audre. (1984). *Sister outsider* (p. 132). New York: The Crossing Press.

Livers, Catherine McGhee. (2003). *Biblical history of Black mankind* (pp. 7-27). Indianapolis: Shahar Publishing.

Lovelace, Earl. (1975). *The dragon can't dance*. London: Longman.

Lyotard, Jean-Francois. (1984). *The postmodern condition: a report on knowledge*, trans. G. Bennington, B. Massumi (p. xxiv). Minneapolis: University of Minnesota Pr.

McDougall, Joyce. (1989). *Theatres of the body: a psychoanalytic approach to psychosomatic illness.* (pp. 32-49). London: Free Association Books.

McGrath, Alister. (1995). *Evangelicalism and the future of Christianity* (p. 116). Downers Grove: Intervarsity.

Mahler, M. S., F. Pine and A. Bergman. (1975). *The psychological birth of the human infant: symbiosis and individuation*. London: Hutchinson.

Malcolm X, with Alex Haley. (2001). *Autobiography* (pp. 318-21). London: Penguin.

Mangalwadi, Ruth/Vishal. (1999). *The legacy of William Carey.* Wheaton: Crossway.

Mang Juan, peasant leader. (1976). Quoted in Charles Avila, *Peasant theology* (p. 13). Bangkok: World Student Christian Federation, Asia region.

Martin-Baro, I. (1994). *Writings for a liberation psychology*. Cambridge: Harvard U.P.

Marx, Karl. (1977). *Capital*, Vol.1, trans. Ben Fowkes (pp. 125, 163, 165). New York: Vintage.

May, Peter. (1990). *Dialogue in evangelism.* Nottingham: Grove Books.

Mayhew, Arthur. (1931). *Christianity and the government of India* (pp. 31, 165-6). London: Faber and Gwyer Ltd.

Mbiti, John S. (1969). *African religions and philosophy* (p. 237). London: Heinemann.

Mbiti, John S. (1970). *Concepts of God in Africa.* London: SPCK.

Mbiti, John S. (1975b). *The prayers of African religion.* London: SPCK.

Metcalf, Thomas. (1964). *The aftermath of revolt – India 1857-1870* (p. 12ff). Princeton: Princeton University Press.

Michel, Otto. (1966). *Brief an die Romer*, ed. MeyersKomm (pp. 75, 254). Gottingen: Vandenhoeck.

Miranda, Jose Porfirio. (1982). *Marx and the Bible: a critique of the philosophy of oppression*, trans. John Eagleson. (pp. xi, 35-200, 36, 83, 93, 107 n.35, n.36, n.37, n.38, 110, 111 ff.). London: SCM Press.

Mirza, Heidi Safia. (2005). 'The more things change, the more they stay the same': assessing Black underachievement 35 years on, in Brian Richardson ed., *Tell it like it is: how our schools fail Black children* (pp. 111-9). London/Stoke-on-Trent: Bookmarks Publications/Trentham Books.

The Missionary Register. (1821). May, p. 179.

Morel, E.D. (1969). *The Black man's burden* (p. 8). New York: Monthly Review Pr.

Morrison, Toni. (1993). *Playing in the dark: whiteness and the literary imagination.* (pp. 4, 5, 11). London: Picado.

Moyo, Dambisa. (2010). *Dead aid.* London: Penguin.

Myers, William H. (2007). Jesus Christ and the poor, in Cain Hope Felder ed., *The Original African Heritage Study Bible* (p. 1578). Valley Forge: Judson Press.

National Centre for Biotechnology Information (2010). *Do US Black women experience stress-related accelerated biological aging? A novel theory and first population-based test of Black-white differences in telomere length.* http://www.ncbi.nlm.nih.gov/pmc/articles/PMC2861506/

National Church Leaders' Forum. (2014). *Black church political mobilization: a manifesto for action.* London: NCLF.

Newton, John. (1788). Thoughts upon the African slave trade. Reprinted in Bernard Martin and Mark Spurrell eds. (1962). *Journal of a slave trader.* London: Epworth.

Noble, Lowell, with Ed Mahoney, Bert Newton and Jill Shook. (2012). Ownership, land and jubilee justice. In Jill Suzanne Shook ed., *Making housing happen: faith-based affordable housing models* (p. 47). Eugene: Wipf and Stock.

Noll, Mark A. (2003). *The rise of evangelicalism: the age of Edwards, Whitefield and the Wesleys* (pp. 19-20, 53-8, 60-70, 100-1, 154). Downers Grove: IVP.

Noll, Mark A. (1994). *The scandal of the evangelical mind* (pp. 83-145). Michigan: Eerdmans.

Noll, Mark A. (2014). *From every tribe and nation.* Grand Rapids: Baker Academic.

North, Christopher R. (1936). Sacrifice in the Old Testament, *Expository Times* 47, no. 6, March, p. 252.

Oakman, Douglas E. (1986). *Jesus and the economic questions of his day* (p. 72). New York: Edwin Mellen Press.

Obama, Barack H. (2007). *Dreams from my father* (pp. 90-1).Edinburgh: Canongate.

Obenga, Theophile. (1989). African philosophy of the Pharaonic period, in Ivan van Sertima ed., *Egypt revisited*. New Brunswick: Transaction.

Oosthuizen, G. C. (1968). *Post-Christianity in Africa – a theological and anthropological study* (p. 235). London: Hurst and Co.

Orr, Deborah. (2014). UK property prices have made us millionaires – but damaged democracy. *The Guardian*, 16th May.

Oxfam policy paper (Sarah Dransfield). (2014). *A tale of two Britains: inequality in the UK*. Oxford: Oxfam.

Oxfam policy paper (Deborah Hardoon). (2015). *Wealth: having it all and wanting more*. Oxford: Oxfam.

Pannell, William. (1989). Is Dr. King on board? In Vinay Samuel and Albrecht Hauser eds., *Proclaiming Christ in Christ's way* (p. 206). Oxford: Regnum.

Parliamentary Papers, 1790-1791, Vol. 92.

Paul, Samuel A. (2009). *The Ubuntu God: Deconstructing a South African narrative of oppression* (Princeton theological monograph). Eugene, OR: Pickwick Pubns.

Pease, Paul. (2005). *Travel with William Carey: the missionary to India who attempted great things for God*. London: Day One Publications.

Perelberg, Rosine, ed. (1999). *Psychoanalytic understanding of violence and suicide*. London: Routledge.

Perkins, Spencer and Chris Rice. (1993). *More than equals: racial healing for the sake of the gospel* (p. 18). Downers Grove: InterVarsity Press.

Perkinson, James W. (2004). *White theology: outing supremacy in modernity* (p. 214). Basingstoke: Palgrave Macmillan.

Philip, T.V. (1987). Christianity in India during Western colonialism, in *The Indian Church History Review*, p. 17. Bangalore: The Church History Association of India.

Philip, T.V. (1999). *Edinburgh to Salvador: twentieth century ecumenical missiology* (ch. 1). Delhi: CSS/ISPCK.

Pinn, Anthony. (2003). *Terror and triumph* (pp. 27-80). Minneapolis: Fortress.

Pregeant, Russell. (1978). *Christology beyond dogma: Matthew's Christ in process hermeneutics* (p. 15). Philadelphia: Fortress.

Rad, Gerhard von. (1966). *Deuteronomy: a commentary*. Philadelphia: Westminster.

Reuben, Anthony. (2015). http://www.bbc.co.uk/news/business-30879173

Reddie, Anthony G. (2014). *Working against the grain: re-imaging Black theology in the 21st century* (p. 17). London: Routledge.

Richard, Pablo et al., *The idols of death and the God of life* (pp. 3-25). Trans. Barbara E. Campbell and Bonnie Shepard. Eugene: Wipf and Stock.

Robert, Dana L. (2000). Shifting Southward: global Christianity since 1945, in *International Bulletin of Missionary Research*, April, pp. 50-8.

Robertson J. and J. Robertson. (1989). *Separation and the very young*. London: Free Association Books.

Rourke, Thomas R. (1996). Michael Novak and Yves R. Simon on the Common Good and Capitalism, in *Review of Politics*, no. 2, Spring 1996, p. 250.

Sanneh, Lamin & Joel A. Carpenter eds. (2005). *The changing face of Christianity*. New York: OUP.

Sanneh, Lamin. (1993). *Encountering the West*. London: Marshall Pickering.

Sanneh, Lamin. (1990). *Translating the message*. New York: Orbis.

Sanneh, Lamin. (2003). *Whose religion is Christianity? The gospel beyond the West* (pp. 1-4). Michigan: Eerdmans.

Sanneh, Lamin. (2008). *Disciples of all nations* (pp. xix-xxii). Oxford: OUP.

Schaeffer, Francis. (2007). *Escape from reason*. Leicester: IVP.

Schaeffer, Francis. (1998). *The God who is there*. Leicester: IVP.

Schaeffer, Francis. (1972). *He is there and He is not silent*. London: Hodder.

Schrenk, G. (1964). *dikaiosune* , in *Kittel's Theological Dictionary of the New Testament* 2 pp. 192 ff., trans. Geoffrey W. Bromiley. Grand Rapids: Eerdmans.

Segundo, Juan Luis. (1976). *The liberation of theology* (p. 95). Maryknoll: Orbis.

Shank, David A. (1986). *William Wade Harris c. 1860-1929,* Harrist Church (Eglise Harriste) Liberia, Ghana, Cote d'Ivoire, in *International Bulletin of Missionary Research*, October, Vol. 10, Issue 4, pp. 170-6.

Sharp, Alan J. (2014). *Changing Generations: challenging power and oppression in Britain today*. London: BIS Publications. www.diversityunity.com

Sider, Ronald J. (2008). For the common good, in *Thinking Biblically about politics*. Grand Rapids: Baker.

Sivanandan, A. (1976). Race, Class & the State: the Black Experience in Britain. *Race & Class*, XVII/4, Spring.

Sivanandan, A. ed. (1982). *Roots of racism*. (p. 6). London: IRR.

Smith, George. (n.d). *The Life of Alexander Duff*. New York: American Tract Society.

Song, Choan-Seng. (1977). *Christian mission in reconstruction: An Asian analysis* (pp. 1-2). Maryknoll: Orbis.

Spirit and power: A 10-country survey of pentecostals (2006). Washington D.C.: Pew Forum on Religion and Public Life, at http://www.pewforum.org

Stott, John R. W. (1992). *The contemporary Christian* (pp. 13, 16-7, 27-9, 110-3, 216). Leicester: IVP.

Stuart, Tristram. (2009). *Waste*. London: Penguin.

Sung, John. (1995). *The Diaries of John Sung – An Autobiography* (pp. 34, 183, 198ff), trans. Stephen L. Sheng. Brighton MI: Luke H. Sheng and Stephen L. Sheng.

Sung, Jung Mo. (2011). *The subject, capitalism and religion: horizons of hope in complex societies*. Basingstoke: Palgrave Macmillan.

Tamez, Elsa. (1993). *The amnesty of grace: justification by faith from a Latin American perspective* (p. 196 n 3), trans. Sharon H. RInge. Nashville: Abingdon.

Tamez, Elsa. (2006). *Bible of the oppressed* (pp. 31-55). Eugene: Wipf and Stock.

Tan, Dr. Kim. (2008). *The jubilee gospel*. Milton Keynes: Authentic Media.

Tawney, R. H. (2013). Poverty as an industrial problem, inaugural lecture. Reproduced in *Memoranda on the problems of poverty* (London: William Morris).

Thandeka. (1999). *Learning to be white* (pp. 20-7). New York: Continuum.

Thiong'O, Ngugi Wa. (1986). Church, culture and politics, in *Homecoming essays on African and Caribbean literature, culture and politics* (p. 32). London: Heinemann.

Thomas, Hugh. (1997). *The slave trade: the history of the Atlantic slave trade 1440-1870*. (pp. 805-6). London: Picador.

Thompson, Thomas. (1772). *The African trade for Negro slaves shown to be consistent with the principles of humanity and the laws of revealed religion*. London.

Turnbull, Richard. (2006). Presentation to 2006 Reform conference. Video at http://video.google.co.uk/videoplay?docid=-6503205096436563217 see also http://www.change.freeuk.com/learning/relthink/turnbull.html

Turner, Harold. (1977). The primal religions of the world and their study, in Victor Hayes (ed.) *Australian essays in world religions.* Bedford Park: Australian Association for World Religions.

United Nations Development Programme. (1999). *1999 human development report*.

United Nations Development Programme. (2007). *2007 human development report*.

VanZanten, Susan. (2014). *Reading a different story: a Christian scholar's journey from America to Africa*. Grand Rapids: Baker Academic.

Vidales, Raul. (1978). *Cristianismo Anti-burgues* (pp. 116-7). San Jose: DEI.

Voth, Steven M. (2003). Justice and/or righteousness: a contextualized analysis of *sedeq* in the KJV (English) and RVR (Spanish). In Glen G. Scorgie, Mark L. Strauss and Steven M. Voth eds., *The challenge of Bible translation: communicating God's word to the world* (pp. 321-45). Grand Rapids: Zondervan.

Walls, Andrew F. (1970). The first chapter of the epistle to the Romans and the modern missionary movement, in W. Ward Gasque and Ralph P. Martin eds., *Apostolic history and the gospel* (Biblical and historical essays presented to F. F. Bruce on his 60th birthday, p. 356). Exeter: Paternoster.

Walls, Andrew F. (1989). *The significance of Christianity in Africa* (The St. Colm's Lecture, 1989, p. 5).

Watkins, Mary and Helene Shulman. (2010). *Toward psychologies of liberation*. Basingstoke: Palgrave Macmillan.

Weinfeld, Moshe. (1992). Justice and righteousness: the expression and its meaning. In Reventlow, Henning Graf and Yair Hoffman eds., *Justice and righteousness: Biblical themes and their influence* (pp. 228-46). Sheffield: JSOT.

West, Carolyn. (2008). Mammy, Jezebel, Sapphire and their homegirls: developing an 'oppositional gaze' toward the images of Black women. In J. Chrisler, C. Golden & P. Rozee eds., *Lectures on the psychology of women*, 4th ed. (pp. 286-99). New York: McGraw Hill.

West, Gerald. (2005). http://theotherjournal.com/2005/08/08/structural-sin-a-south-african-perspective/

Westermann, Claus. (1969). *Isaiah 40-66: a commentary* (pp. 54-6, 59, 133 n.32, 337). Philadelphia: Westminster Press.

Westermann, Dietrich. (1937). *Africa and Christianity* (Duff Lectures 1935, pp. 2, 94). London: OUP.

Westermann, Dietrich. (1926). The value of the African's past, in *International Review of Missions*, XV, p. 426.

Wilcock, Michael. (1979). *The Saviour of the world: the message of Luke's gospel* (pp. 76, 86). Leicester: IVP.

Wilkinson, Guy, on behalf of the Mission and Public Affairs Council. (2005). *Presence and Engagement: the churches' task in a multi faith society*, GS 1577 (pp. 35, 88 n 13). London: The Archbishops' Council.

Wilkinson, Richard and Kate Pickett. (2010). *The spirit level*. London: Penguin.

Williams, Eric. (1940). The golden age of the slave system in Britain. In *Journal of Negro History*, Vol. 25, no. 1, January.

Williams, Eric. (1994). *Capitalism and slavery*. (pp. 3-30). Chapel Hill: The University of North Carolina Press.

Williamson, S. G. (1965). *Akan religion and the Christian faith* (p. 168). Accra: Ghana Universities Press.

Winnicott, D. W. (1984). *Deprivation and delinquency*. London: Routledge.

Wolterstorff, Nicholas P. (2010). *Justice: Rights and Wrongs* (pp. 110-3). Princeton: Princeton University Press.

Wolterstorff, Nicholas P. (2013). *Journey toward justice: personal encounters in the global South*. Grand Rapids: Baker Academic.

Woods, Scott. (2014). http://scottwoodsmakeslists.wordpress.com/2014/01/03/5-things-no-one-is-actually-saying-about-ani-difranco-or-plantations/ .

Woodson, Carter G. (1977). *The mis-education of the Negro* (p. xiii). Washington D.C.: Associated Publishers.

World conference on church and society. (1967). July 12-26. Geneva: WCC.

World Bank. (2008). *World development indicators*.

World Christian Database Centre. (2013). Todd M. Johnson et al., *Christianity in its global context, 1970-2020: society, religion and mission*. Society for the study of global Christianity at Gordon-Conwell Theological Seminary.

Wright, N. T. (Tom). (1992). *The New Testament and the people of God* (pp. 10, 60, 88, 92-5). London: SPCK.

Wright, N. T. (Tom). (1996). *Jesus and the victory of God* (pp. 13-5, 179, 615-31). London: SPCK.

Wright, N. T. (Tom). (2011). *Surprised by hope* (pp. 201-33). London: SPCK.

Wright, Richard. (1964). *White man listen!* (p. 6). New York: Anchor Books.

Yancey, George. (1998). *Reconciliation theology: results of a multiracial evangelical community*. Paper presented at the *Color lines in the twenty-first century* conference, Chicago, Illinois.

Young, Edward J. (1971). *The book of Isaiah* (Vol. 1. pp. 325, 344). Grand Rapids: Eerdmans.

Yu, Carver T. (1988). *Being and relation: a theological critique of Western dualism and individualism*. Edinburgh: Scottish Academic Press.

Zimmerli, Walter. (1964). *pais Theou* in Kittel's Theological Dictionary of the New Testament, trans. and ed. Geoffrey W. Bromiley (5: 669). Grand Rapids: Eerdmans.

Glossary

Binary opposition. A situation that is reducible to two possible answers that are mutually exclusive, or any situation that has only two possible outcomes that are mutually exclusive. These two answers or outcomes oppose each other. They are also used in a way that privileges one of the pair at the expense of the other.

Contextualisation. To make a positive use of material from the people groups in question to demonstrate not only that conversion to Christ from this background is appropriate but also that the true insights from these people groups' traditions converge on Christ (Bediako, 1999).

Diaspora. The scattered population of people with a common origin in a different area.

Dualism. Traditionally, two elements that are seen as being in binary opposition to one another, one seen to be good and the other bad, e.g. mind and body, men and women, next world and this world.

Enslavement. The process by which a person was brought into slavery, a condition where they were treated as property and forced to work. Enslavement indicates that people have a history, culture, identity, etc. prior to slavery and are not defined by slavery.

Hendiadys. This is the use of two nouns (for example, 'justice' and 'right') for greater effect on the reader, when the meaning is one of these nouns as an adjective modifying the other noun. In this example, that would be 'right justice' or 'social justice'.

Meta-narratives. According to Lyotard, is any narrative that seeks to justify its claims by using universal, autonomous reason.

Synonymous parallelism. A figure of speech used in Hebrew poetry, where the words in the first line of a verse seem to be repeated very similarly in the second line of the verse. E.g. 'The earth is the Lord's and the fullness thereof:
the world, and all they that dwell therein' (Ps. 24: 1). The phrase "is the Lord's" doesn't appear in the second colon but is implied: this is known as an ellipsis. In synonymous parallelism, it would probably be a mistake to interpret the

colons/phrases as if they were communicating distinctly different meanings from each other.

Index

Lightning Source UK Ltd.
Milton Keynes UK
UKOW07f2225250815

257528UK00010B/260/P